Orphan
of
Islam

Orphan of Islam

No one will listen. No one will help.

Alexander Khan

HARPER

HARPER

An Imprint of HarperCollins*Publishers*
77–85 Fulham Palace Road,
Hammersmith, London W6 8JB

www.harpercollins.co.uk

First published by HarperCollins*Publishers* 2012

1 3 5 7 9 10 8 6 4 2

© Alexander Khan 2012

Alexander Khan asserts the moral right to
be identified as the author of this work

A catalogue record of this book is
available from the British Library

ISBN 978-0-00-744478-6

Printed and bound in Great Britain by
Clays Ltd, St Ives plc

MIX
Paper from
responsible sources
FSC™
www.fsc.org   **FSC˚ C007454**

FSC™ is a non-profit international organisation established to promote
the responsible management of the world's forests. Products carrying the
FSC label are independently certified to assure customers that they come
from forests that are managed to meet the social, economic and
ecological needs of present and future generations,
and other controlled sources.

Find out more about HarperCollins and the environment at
www.harpercollins.co.uk/green

I dedicate this book to Abad.
Without his help I would not be here.
And to my wife Jessica –
I love you very much.

JALALABAD

AFGHAN/PAKISTAN BORDER

MADRASSA AREA

PESHAWAR CITY

G TR

INDUS RIVER

TAJAK

WALK BACK TO VILLAGE

GREAT TRUNK ROAD

KAMRA AIR FORCE BASE

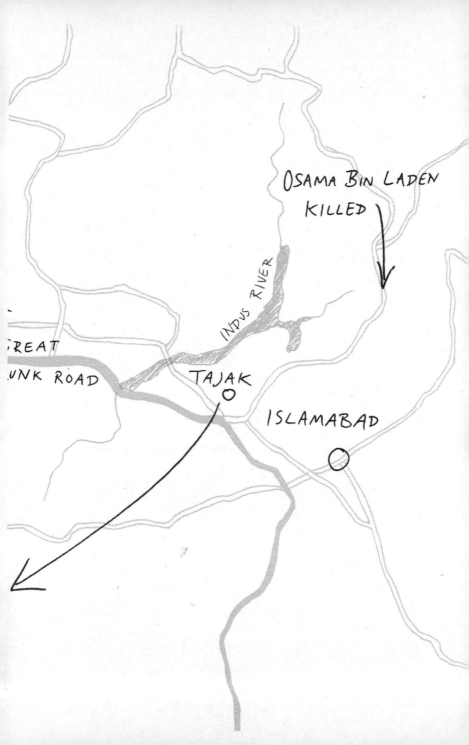

Acknowledgments

I would like to thank my wife Jessica, who I first shared my story with. As the torrent of truth spilled out of me she didn't reject or ridicule me. She just sat there and listened, and when I had finished she said she understood.

I would also like to thank Jessica's mum and dad for always being there for me.

A big thank you to my agent, Euan Thorneycroft at AM Heath, for his continued guidance and assistance, but most of all for believing that I had a story to share.

I would like to thank Tom, who has supported my journey at all times. Without his help this book would not have been written.

A huge thank you to Joan for finding my mother.

Further thanks go to Steven McLaughlin, author of *Squaddie: A Soldier's Story* for his support and advice.

I will forever be grateful to all the team at HarperCollins for putting this book together. In particular I would like to thank Victoria McGeown who immediately saw the potential to tell my story.

Author's Note

I hope my story is inspirational for those who might find themselves in similar situations and think there is no hope and no way out. There is always a way out, even when the odds are stacked against you and the wall seems very high.

I've been there, scared, not knowing who to ask for help. It's not a nice feeling.

www.alexander-khan.co.uk is a website that offers confidential help and advice to people in similar situations to those described in this book.

Prologue

T he mullah bends down, his long grey-black beard brush-ing against my feet as he unlocks the leg brace. I've been standing rigid in it for at least three hours, unable to sit, kneel or even squat for fear of snapping my ankles. I could cry with relief, but I'm too frightened to cry. At least not yet.

He points to the blackboard in front of me with his bamboo stick, the one he uses to whack us all with when we can't pronounce something from the Holy Book. My Arabic is rubbish; I'm very used to that stick.

'Read it,' he commands, glaring at me with dark eyes.

All the lights have gone out across the madrassa and the only illumination in the room is a lantern with a tiny wick. I read the chalked scripture slowly, trying to pronounce all the words right:

'*La ilaha illallah Muhammad rasul Allah*' ('There is no God but Allah, and Muhammad is His Messenger.')

Whack! The stick comes across my shoulders. Wrong again. Hearing Arabic spoken is one thing, trying to read it quite another, and my northern English accent easily wins out. The mullah glares at me with undisguised contempt.

'Go back to your room,' he says. 'We'll see each other in here again tomorrow. You're a disgrace to Islam.'

I stumble through the darkness to the dormitory and feel my way across the room to my blanket. Most of the boys are sleeping. I lie down and start to cry, as quietly as I can. The question goes through my mind, the same question that nags me night and day: how the hell have I ended up here? An ordinary lad from Lancashire stuck in some kind of weird medieval fairy story, but with no sign of a happy ending …

Back home, my mates are secretly listening to Bros or Guns n' Roses in their bedrooms, hoping their dads won't catch them and send them for an extra session of prayer at the mosque. That is as bad as life gets for them; why have I been singled out for such harsh punishment so far from home? What have I done to deserve this?

Chapter One

I see a face, a white face, but I don't recall any features other than dark eyes and a smile. What I remember most is her long dark hair. As she bends down, it tickles the sides of my cheeks and I laugh. She laughs too, then the sun comes out and streams through the thin curtains of the living room. She turns away and is gone. This is the only memory of my mum I have from childhood.

I've no idea what she was like as a mother during those brief first few years. I can't recall the stories she told, the food she cooked, the games she played or even the sound of her voice. There is no scent in this world that evokes her smell, no object or place that brings back those precious moments in time. Dark hair and a white face are all I have, and while that hasn't been much, it has been enough to hang on to in my worst moments. I always knew she was out there somewhere, even when she'd apparently vanished from the face of the Earth. All I wanted was her to come back and take us home.

What I know about Margaret Firth is what I've pieced together over the years and what I've learned more recently. She was born near Manchester, the youngest of three sisters living in a house of poverty and pain. Her parents had little time or regard for her. Although she looked up to her sisters, it wasn't the easiest of relationships. When her elder siblings moved out and made lives for themselves she would go to live with them from time to time, returning to her parents' home when they'd had enough of her. It was a lonely life, back and forth between people who didn't really want her. Her parents worked in the textile industry. Margaret would eventually do the same, getting a job in a local mill as soon as she left school.

My father, Ahmed Khan, was born in the village of Tajak, in the Attock district of north-west Pakistan. It is a rural and deeply religious area not far from the North-West Frontier and the border with Afghanistan. Ahmed was the eldest of five siblings: three brothers and two sisters. For the first 30 or so years of his life he lived pretty much how people have lived in this area, close to the Indus river, for many years. The men rise before dawn and go to the mosque for prayers. They return home to walled compounds containing several houses occupied by members of the extended family. Their wives are already up and have prayed in their living rooms on a mat facing Mecca. Then it is into the kitchen to cook curry and chapatis. The food is placed in a small clay pot with a lid on and given to the men as they head out for a day working in the *harat*, or field. Each family has its own plot of land, irrigated by a large well and including a small brick hut containing tools. Many men spend their entire lives in this routine, their faces etched with deep lines by the sun. Others become drivers or co-drivers of the trucks and buses that travel ceaselessly across Pakistan and beyond. Some turn into mechanics and set up their own garages; others open grocers' shops. In these rural villages the women just stay at home, raise children and keep house. They are not allowed to do much else.

But even in these insular communities there are men who seek something else. My father was one of them. His eldest sister, Fatima, had travelled to England with her husband, Dilawar, and set up a shop in a mill town in Lancashire. Letters came to Ahmed telling of a wonderful island where the sea was close by and earnings were three, four and five times the amount they were in the village. Fatima revelled in her status as an emigrant adventurer and encouraged her older brother to follow suit.

In the late 1960s the only way for a poor Pakistani to travel to England was by road. It was a 25-day journey across difficult terrain and through inhospitable countries. Dad made an attempt but was delayed in Karachi and his money ran out. It didn't put him off; he went home, saved up and within a year tried again. This time he succeeded and, after spending time earning money on construction projects in Germany, arrived in England just before the end of the 1960s, with many other Pakistani, Indian and Caribbean immigrants.

Dad went straight up to Lancashire and to the Hawesmill area of the town his sister was living in. Hawesmill was built in the late nineteenth century to house large numbers of mill workers cheaply. Streets lined with stone-built terrace houses stretched for hundreds of yards up steep, windswept hills, forming a tightly-knit enclave that seemed forbidding to outsiders. By the time Dad arrived, many of its white inhabitants had gone for good. Cotton was no longer a major industry in Lancashire – although some mills were still working – and Hawesmill's rundown old housing had almost served its purpose. But not quite, for a new set of people had moved in, and were finding the natural insularity of the place to their liking. Bengalis, Punjabis, Sindhis and Pathans were making Hawesmill their own, laying down roots and traditions founded in far-off villages. To the rest of the town, they were just 'them Pakis'.

My father was a Pathan, one of a light-skinned and tall race of people who originate from Afghanistan and north-west Pakistan and speak Pashto. They were part of the Persian Empire and throughout history were known to be fierce warriors, defeating everyone who dared invade their lands, from Alexander the Great to the Soviet Union. As we know, they are still fighting today and are a strict, unyielding and deeply religious people. That said, they are also warm and if you befriend a Pathan, it's for life.

Fatima was keen to help out her brother and persuaded her husband that he should have a job in his shop. Dad worked there for a while, but the wages were low and it was a matter of pride that he sent money back to the family in Tajak. He left the shop and found a job in a mill in Bolton that took on immigrants prepared to work for lower wages than white people.

He lived in a terrace house with four other men, all Pathans from the same area, and they hot-bedded: when one was on a night shift another would sleep in the bed, then vacate it to go to work when the night worker came home. If there was a time when they were all together, they would sit in the front room of the house, smoke cigarettes and play cards and talk about work and how they missed Pakistan. They would only go home, they declared, once they'd made enough money to build a house in their village. In winter they would pull worn-out second-hand coats over their traditional *salwar kameez* clothing when they went outdoors and learn not to moan too much about the wind and rain coming in off the bleak moors. Lancashire wasn't home, and would never be, but when they talked and listened to Pathan music, home didn't seem so far away. 'Only a few more years,' they'd promise themselves before heading off to the mosque – a couple of terrace houses knocked into one. Men from all over Hawesmill would squeeze into it five times a day. This was the reality of Dad's adventure in England, day after day after day.

No wonder, then, that his curiosity was aroused when a young Englishwoman caught his eye during his shift at the mill. He didn't know any white people and he couldn't speak much English. He saw no reason to mix; from what he'd heard, whites didn't like Pakistanis 'coming in and taking all the jobs'. But this woman seemed different. She smiled at him, and it was genuine. Shyly he looked away, then back again. She was still smiling.

'Hiya,' she said, 'what's your name?'

He shrugged, not understanding. But a Bengali friend working on the same shift could speak half-decent English and caught the question.

'Hey,' he said to Dad, 'the girl's asking your name. Aren't you going to tell her? She's a pretty one. Go on, tell her …'

Dad smiled, but said nothing. Farouk leaned round the spinning loom and shouted to the girl, 'It's Ahmed … Yeah, Ahmed. He likes you. Talk to him.'

Margaret Firth, 18, lonely and lacking confidence, liked her Asian co-workers. They seemed quiet and dignified, never complaining like the local Bolton lads or drinking and messing about. She appreciated how respectful they were when they spoke to her. And there was something she really liked about Ahmed, even if he couldn't hold much of a conversation.

Dad was a village boy, but he wasn't daft. He'd made it to England, found work and was sending money home. He missed Pakistan, but he certainly didn't want to go back. Not yet. What better way to stay than to marry an Englishwoman? It would give him residency and maybe take him out of Hawesmill altogether. The idea of marrying someone from a non-Muslim background would horrify his sister and the Pathan communities in both Hawesmill and Tajak, but no matter. He would bring her into Islam, and Fatima would teach her the ways of Pakistani women. It would be fine.

Now, I don't really know if this was the case or not. Perhaps Dad got together with Mum out of love. He certainly liked her enough to introduce her to the family in Hawesmill, braving the stares and whispers that she must have attracted. Mum seemed happy to go along with whatever he wanted. For the first time in her life she'd found someone who treated her with kindness and respect. She was young and impressionable. The language, the clothing, the customs and the cooking all baffled her at first, but when Dad asked her to live with him in a rented terrace house she agreed immediately. They had a formal *nika*, or engagement ceremony, performed by the local imam. She dressed the way Dad wanted and learned to cook the food he liked. He tried to improve his English. Maybe they would be alright.

Dad's sister didn't think so. Fatima was against the relationship from the start and was horrified when they set up home together. It was *haraam*, strictly forbidden in Islamic law, and a source of dishonour. Fatima was a pioneer, the first of her family to live in England. Her word was law. Ahmed was bringing shame on her and Dilawar around Hawesmill. Again and again she begged him to leave the Englishwoman. Dad was having none of it. Mum's parents didn't want anything to do with her, so they eloped to Scotland, where there were jobs waiting for them in a textile mill in Perth, and finally married up there.

I was born on 22 February 1975 and named Mohammed Abdul Khan. My sister, Jasmine, was born in March the following year. Dad was now the father of two British-born children and was entitled to stay in the country for as long as he liked.

What happened next is unclear. There are stories of Dad starting to get a taste for whisky – also completely *haraam* under Islamic law. Never having drunk alcohol in his life, he became aggressive. I've been told he started hitting Mum while drunk. Perhaps he found being married to a Westerner and fathering two children with her much harder than he had expected. Maybe he missed Hawesmill or even Tajak.

What I do know is that within a relatively short space of time, the four of us were back in the north-west of England. Mum and Dad rented a house in Bury, picking up jobs in what remained of the rapidly declining textile industry. Dad seemed pleased to be closer to his family again, but his happiness wasn't shared by Mum. Fatima was now openly hostile towards her, shunning her when we went to visit and speaking in Pashto to confuse her.

Dad was the source of more grief. He'd stopped drinking, but was now disappearing from the house for days and even weeks on end. 'Family business at home,' Mum was told. In this case, 'home' meant Pakistan. Without explanation or apology, Dad would just pack a suitcase and go. Mum would be left with two children in a damp, rented terrace house, with no idea when he would come back.

One morning in desperation she put us in the pram, got the bus to Hawesmill and walked up the steep street to Fatima's house, determined to find out what her husband was up to.

'Is he here?' she demanded, as Fatima opened the door. 'Or is he back in Pakistan? I've got two little kids here who miss their dad. I know you don't like me. But I've a right to know what's going on.'

Fatima paused. She had no time for this *kuffar*, this unbeliever, who had brought shame on her. But she felt that she *was* entitled to an explanation. Maybe if she heard the truth, she would disappear very quickly. She invited Mum to come in and sit down.

'You should hear this from Ahmed, not me,' said Fatima. 'But since he's not here I may as well tell you – the reason he goes to Pakistan all the time is because of his family.'

'I know that,' said Mum. 'But if he's so desperate to see his mum and dad, or his brothers, sisters, aunties, cousins, whoever, then why doesn't he just bring them over here for a visit?'

Fatima smiled. The poor woman was clueless.

'Not that sort of family,' she said. 'Ahmed has a wife in Tajak. He married her before he married you. Oh, they've got a few children too.'

I wonder what Mum thought as she wandered in a daze back to the bus station that day, the hems of her badly fitting *salwar kameez* trousers trailing through puddle-strewn cobbled streets, with two scruffy mixed-race kids crying in the pram. Meanwhile, somewhere hot, somewhere she'd never been invited for now obvious reasons, Dad was enjoying the fruits of his labours with the family he'd kept secret from her.

I was too young to remember the row that took place when Dad finally got home. It must have been one hell of a ding-dong. I imagine Mum screwing her Asian clothes up into a ball and throwing them at him, then telling him to cook his own bloody lentil dhal. It sounds almost comic, like a scene from *East Is East*, but it must have been awful. However it was conducted and whatever was said, the upshot was that Dad moved out of our house and into Fatima's, leaving Mum with custody of the pair of us.

Now I believe Fatima acted maliciously by telling Mum the truth about Dad. She wanted to split them up. But in a way Mum had what she wanted – two beautiful children to care for and love as she had never been loved. She didn't have to fit in with foreign customs anymore or cook funny food. She had a roof over her head and a job. There were people saying, 'Told you so,' but she didn't care. I'd like to think that my first memory of her happened around this point: her smiling face turned towards me and the sun coming out.

'Mohammed, oh my Mohammed …' Do I remember her whispering that as she cuddled me protectively to her? Perhaps she did. At any rate, I'd like to think she was happy.

Dad still wanted to see us and would call round at weekends. Mum was still angry with him, but didn't stop him from visiting. I guess he wouldn't have taken us much further than the local park or the ice-cream parlour, and up to Hawesmill to see the family. Whether they wanted to see us would have been another matter, but knowing Dad he would've made sure that the family connections so important to Muslims were maintained, even if they included the children of an unbeliever.

One Saturday in the early part of 1978, just a few months after Dad and Mum had split up, he called for us as usual. He made sure we were dressed in our best clothes and also had a change of outfit. He explained to Mum that there was a family gathering in Hawesmill because a relative had flown in from Pakistan. We needed a change of clothes, he said, because we'd end up playing in the backyard and would get filthy. Mum packed us a little bag each, kissed us both on the head and saw us to the door. I guess we turned and waved to her as we climbed into the back of the battered old Datsun Dad always borrowed to pick us up. She shut the door, happy that she had a few hours to herself before we returned, tired out, after a long afternoon's playing with the local kids in Hawesmill.

In the 1970s only lucky little English kids travelled on aeroplanes. Normally a family like ours would've been completely out of the international air travel league, but strong ties to Pakistan meant that money was somehow found to make the trip 'back home' and see relatives longing to hear stories about the land of opportunity that was giving such a warm welcome to its former 'colonials'. I expect there was a whip-round in the streets of Hawesmill in the weeks before Dad came to pick us up from Mum's. Whatever work Dad was doing at the time – shifts in the mill, plus a bit of labouring on the side – wouldn't have paid for three airline tickets to Islamabad. That said, two of those tickets were one-way only, so maybe there was a discount. I don't know – I'd just turned three and Jasmine was almost two. Babies, really – and far too young to be removed from their mother without explanation.

From what I can gather, the police were involved. I'd like to think that Mum banged on every door in Hawesmill for answers. She certainly did later on, until it became clear that she wasn't going to get a straight answer out of anyone up there. But what were the police's chances of making an arrest? An Asian man takes his mixed-race kids to Pakistan for a holiday and forgets to tell his estranged wife, a white woman who tried to fit in with the funny foreigners but wasn't welcome – sounds like an open-and-shut case. Perhaps the police thought she had it coming to her, or maybe they did try hard to find us. But the trail would've gone cold as soon as we arrived in Islamabad, and I don't think the law could've expected much help in Hawesmill.

We were taken to Tajak for a 'holiday' and put in the care of various 'aunties', some related, some not. Dad stayed for a while, a week or two perhaps, then went back to England. The need to earn money must have been overwhelming, because of course he had two families to support, so staying in Pakistan for any length of time wasn't an option.

Meanwhile Mum made repeated attempts to track us down, without success. She must have been heartbroken, trailing those windswept terrace streets for her two missing children and begging Fatima for news of our whereabouts. What did they tell her – if anything? Many years later, I was told she had been informed by Dad's family that we'd been killed in a car crash while on holiday in Pakistan, and that we'd been buried there. What a terrible thing to say to a mother, especially when it was a barefaced lie. Mum, poor and isolated from her own friends and family, could do nothing to disprove it. Luckily, she never believed it.

I can't recall if I met my step-family at this time. It's probable, given that Tajak is a small place, but being so young, I don't have any memory of them. What I do remember is the day I was circumcised. Although it isn't mentioned in the Qu'ran, circumcision (*tahara*) is a long-established ritual in Islam. It is to do with cleanliness and purification, particularly before prayer, and there was no reason why I would be exempted. Unfortunately for me, Mum had opposed this after my birth and Dad had no choice but to postpone it. Now she wasn't around he could do what he liked, and one of his first jobs in Tajak was to find somebody suitably qualified to do it.

It goes without saying there was no anaesthetic. Dad would've rounded up the village imam, who also served as the village doctor, and a few of the elders, to oversee proceedings. I don't recall their solemn bearded faces leaning over me as I lay on a scruffy bit of carpet in the village mosque, but I do remember the searing pain as the razor-sharp butcher's knife cut through my little foreskin and my blood staining the carpet a deep red. Iodine must've been applied very quickly, as I remember looking down and seeing my genitals covered all over with a substance the colour of saffron. For days afterwards I suffered burning agony when I tried to pee. If I called out for my mummy at any time during those hazy, fractured few years, it would have been then.

My only other memory from this period is when I tried to shoot the moon. I'd found an old pellet gun in the house where we were staying and had been encouraged to take it outside and learn to use it. Having a gun in Pakistan is no big deal and boys handle weapons from an early age. Seeing an old shotgun propped against the interior wall of a house or an AK47 left in the corner of a mosque while its owner says his prayers isn't uncommon. So the uncles of the family must've been delighted when I picked up the gun and lugged it outside. The moon was an obvious target. I'd never seen such clear skies in my short life; the sheer number and brilliance of the stars in the night sky was mesmerizing, and the moon hung in between them like a gigantic waxy-yellow fruit. I heaved the rifle to my shoulder, assisted by Jasmine, and took careless aim at the sky. No one had told me about recoil, so when I dropped it immediately after it went it off, the butt landed right on Jasmine's foot, leaving her with a deep cut and a permanent scar.

We didn't go to school during our time in Pakistan. Our family in England spoke Pashto among themselves, so it's not as if we knew nothing of the language and couldn't have managed to some extent in school. But I imagine the Pakistani relatives thought there was little point in sending us; we probably seemed happy enough, playing in the dust beneath the brick and mud walls of the houses or watching the farmers slowly gather in their crops under the vast and cloudless sky. The days were endless and dangers were few. My Pashto was certainly getting better, and after a year or so I could communicate with my cousins. If Dad hadn't needed to earn money in England, maybe this is where my story would've ended. I'd have remained in Pakistan all my life, tending the fields or driving trucks or fixing cars or keeping a shop. In time the memories of Mum would've faded, and although I might never have fitted in – the gossip about the boy with the *kuffar* for a mother was unlikely to disappear – I'd have probably had an arranged marriage with a cousin and spawned a few kids. The opportunities to do anything other than conform would've been extremely limited. However, it might have been a much happier existence than the one that was waiting for me.

After spending three years in Pakistan, not knowing who we were or if we really belonged to anyone, we were taken back to England. That's when my troubles really began.

Chapter Two

We were met at Heathrow by a gaggle of relatives who'd obviously relished the chance of getting out of Hawesmill for the day, even if it was just a boring trip down the M6 to London. What little baggage we had was crammed into the back of an ancient Ford Transit minibus and we were squashed in against our cousins. They sniggered and winked at one another whenever we spoke in fluent accentless Pashto.

I was jammed up against the window. It was December 1981. The minibus's windscreen wipers waved monotonously the whole journey. It was only late afternoon, but already every headlight was on. England seemed cold, grey and dark. I shivered in my thin *salwar kameez*, wishing I had a nice parka with fur round the hood, just like my cousins had. The endless sun and long, lazy days seemed far away. The further north we travelled, the darker it got. It was like entering the mouth of a tunnel with no end in sight.

'Where's our house?' I asked Dad. 'Where are we going to live? Will Mum be there?'

Dad, sitting in the front passenger seat, turned round and exchanged a glance with Fatima, who was in the aisle seat opposite mine, her two youngest children curled up on her lap. She nodded, then stared at me wordlessly.

'You're going to live with Aunty Fatima for a while,' Dad said. 'Just while I get sorted out. It won't be long before we have our own house. Aunty will look after you until then.'

'But where will you be?'

'I'm busy, Mohammed,' Dad said. 'You'll both have to be patient. I'll be around, off and on. You'll be fine.'

'So when will we see Mum?'

'That's enough questions!' shouted Fatima, sitting upright and glaring at me. 'We don't know where she's gone. So stop asking. You'll be fine with us. Now go to sleep.'

Fatima turned away and pulled her two children closer to her. I traced my finger over the steamed-up window and made a small square that I could see out of. I felt very uncomfortable. Fatima had snapped at me just because I'd asked about Mum. It seemed clear that she wasn't to be mentioned in her presence. But why? Adults were stupid, always telling you not to say this, not to do that. I drew a circle on the window and put in two dots for eyes and a straight line for a nose. I sneaked a look at Fatima, then drew a sad mouth. Already I hated her.

The Transit began a slow crawl from the town centre up to Hawesmill. My memories of this place were few; compared to the spacious compounds in Tajak and the vast fertile plains of the Indus Valley, Hawesmill looked small, cold and mean. Every house was the same. One street was no different from the next. The van bumped and slid over greasy cobbles before stopping outside a house three-quarters of the way up a long terrace row.

'Here we are, kids,' said Dad, smiling. '97 Nile Street. Welcome home. Come on, let's get your stuff in.'

Dad grabbed our bags and gave a few notes to the driver. We stood shivering on the pavement. Snow was falling. I'd never seen white stuff dropping from the sky before and I was rooted to the spot with amazement.

Fatima was busy with her girls, Majeeda, who was 12, and Maisa, aged seven. Her nine-year-old boy, Tamam, banged on the door and shouted through the letterbox. Fatima pulled him away sharply, clipping him on his ear before rummaging in her bag for a key. Tamam winced and stared up at her like a beaten dog. Then he caught me looking at him and pulled his face into a snarl.

Fatima opened the door and pushed us all inside. We crowded into a narrow lobby, tripping over coats, bags and shoes. Tamam and Maisa bustled past Jasmine and me. Tamam gave me an extra shove as he passed.

'Ayesha! Ayesha!' Fatima yelled up the stairs. 'Ayesha, come down now! Have you made the dinner? I can't smell anything. Get down these stairs now!'

A teenage girl stuck her head round the top of the bannister rail and caught my eye. She winked and smiled. She plodded slowly downstairs, even as her mother screeched at her.

'Hurry up, girl,' Fatima said, 'we're all starving. I hope you've made something. Where's your father?'

'At the shop,' she replied. 'Where else? So ... these are the little village kids. Haven't they grown up? They're really brown, too. You'd never think their mum was ...'

'Shut up!' said Fatima fiercely. 'Where's the dinner?'

'Made ages ago,' came the surly reply. 'It's gone cold.'

'Put the stove on then,' Fatima said. 'And leave a plate aside for your father. He'll want something when he comes in.'

Ayesha took our hands and led us into the kitchen. 'What've they been feeding you out there?' she said. 'Goat and more goat, I reckon. Come on, I've made some mincemeat with potatoes and peas. That'll warm you up. Do you want a chapati while you're waiting?'

We nodded, still trying to get used to the sound of Pashto underpinned by flat Lancashire vowels. Ayesha lit the hob and placed the cooking pot on top, then started singing in English.

'Da da, da da, da da, da-da, tainted love, woah-oh, tainted love!' She danced around the tiny kitchen, banging a spatula on the work surface to the rhythm of the song. We looked at her, wide-eyed in amazement. We hadn't heard any music at all in Pakistan. No one ever sang or danced like this.

'Guess what?' Ayesha whispered. 'I've got a radio in my bedroom. It's true – Parveen in Alma Street lent it me. It's got an earphone so no one knows you're listening. I like the charts on a Sunday night. Do you like them too? What's your favourite song? I like Soft Cell, Duran Duran, the Human League – all of them. You can have a listen if you want.'

'Thank you,' I said, not knowing what I'd agreed to.

'It's OK. Just don't tell Mum. I'll get done if she finds out ...'

'Finds out what?' Fatima was standing at the kitchen door, glaring at her 15-year-old daughter. She must've been listening in when Ayesha was singing.

She turned to me. 'What's she been saying to you? Tell me.'

'I dunno,' I said, trying not to look at Ayesha. 'I couldn't understand it.'

'Of course you couldn't,' Fatima said sarcastically. Then she pointed at Ayesha. 'If I catch you singing that rubbish again, I'll put you out of this house. Nice Pakistani girls don't sing. Is that clear?'

Ayesha looked at the floor, then silently turned her back on her mother and stirred the contents of the pot.

'Upstairs, you two,' Fatima said to me and Jasmine, 'and I'll show you where you're sleeping. It'll be a squash, but you'll just have to get used to it.'

The house was tiny: two rooms and a kitchen downstairs and two bedrooms and a bathroom upstairs. For a couple with one child, it would've been just about adequate. But not for two adults and seven children. Yasir, Fatima and Dilawar's elder son, slept in the downstairs front room. He was due to get married in a few months and would then move out, but for the moment he was living at home and working in the family shop with his dad. Fatima and Dilawar slept in the front bedroom upstairs. The back bedroom was shared by Ayesha, Tamam, Majeeda and Maisa. And now there were two more occupants.

Fatima indicated Tamam's bed. 'You're in there,' she said, 'and your sister can get in with Majeeda and Maisa. Yes?'

Jasmine pulled at my sleeve. 'I don't like it here, Moham,' she said. 'It smells funny. I don't want to share a bed. Why can't we go with Dad?'

'Because you can't,' snapped Fatima in her shrill high-pitched voice. The tone of that voice, forever shrieking and shouting around that tiny house, would grate on me in the months ahead. Even now, if I close my eyes I can still hear it, like fingernails going down a blackboard.

'This isn't a hotel,' Fatima continued, 'despite what your father seems to think. Anyway, he's not going to be around for a while, so I'm in charge. And in this house, what I say goes. Got it?'

We nodded meekly.

Fatima threw our pathetic little suitcases onto the beds. 'Dinner will be ready in 10 minutes,' she said, walking out of the bedroom. 'Get your hands and faces washed now.'

That first evening in Nile Street was awful. Dilawar and Yasir knew we were coming to stay, but made no effort to make us feel welcome when they arrived home from the shop. All they wanted was their dinner, and they didn't seem at all happy to have to share it with two new mouths on the other side of the table. But Dad was there, so they said nothing. Fatima was all smiles in front of Dad, reassuring him that of course she'd look after us and yes, we'd be fine staying there and the other kids would love to have two new people to play with. The sly looks and digs in the ribs we were getting from around that cramped table suggested otherwise. Only Ayesha seemed to understand how weird it felt for us to be back in England. She rubbed our heads and gave us extra little pieces of chapati when she thought no one was looking.

'We might make a half-decent Pakistani wife out of you after all,' commented Fatima, who had noticed the extra attention she was giving us.

When the meal was over, the men and a few of the children, me and Jasmine included, sat in the back room. Fatima, Ayesha and Majeeda stayed in the kitchen to clean up. The men lit cigarettes, sat back on the settees, which faced each other along two walls, and chatted among themselves. There was no TV set, so we played on the floor.

After a while, Dad stood up. 'Time I was off,' he said, looking at his watch.

He bent down and kissed us both.

'Now, you two behave for your Aunty Fatima and Uncle Dilawar,' he said. 'I'll be gone for a few weeks now. I've got some work on. Remember, be good. No playing up.'

He shook hands with Dilawar and Yasir and shouted a goodbye to Fatima. The front door banged and he was gone.

Again we were alone. With family, yes, but without the parents we needed and wanted to hold us, look after us, keep us safe.

The false smile Fatima had put on for Dad soon disappeared. The shrill tone was again present in her voice when she ordered us all upstairs to get washed and changed for bed. There were the usual bedtime moans and groans from her children, but Fatima was having none of it. We were hustled up the narrow staircase to the bedroom, Tamam and Majeeda leading the charge.

Majeeda was first into the bathroom, banging the door. Tamam stood outside, shouting and shouting for his sister to hurry up. In the bedroom, Maisa flung Jasmine's suitcase on the floor and climbed onto the bed, stretching out her legs in a defiant display of ownership. Finally, Majeeda left the bathroom and got into bed, pushing Maisa against the wall. There was barely a ruler's width of space for poor Jasmine. She looked at me with frightened eyes and I squeezed her hand. I was just as afraid, but didn't want to let her know.

Tamam came into the room. He looked as though he'd rather share a bed with a crocodile.

'Get in,' he ordered, 'and move right up. If you even breathe, I'll boot you one!'

I did as I was told and squeezed myself as far as I could against the wall. I stared at the cheap torn lime-green wallpaper for as long as possible until the light went off. I was tired from the long flight and journey up from Heathrow, and soon fell asleep. Less than an hour later the light pinged on again. There was no lampshade, and the bare bulb seemed to penetrate every corner of that tiny claustrophobic bedroom.

'Who's nicked my radio?! Come on, you're not going back to sleep till you tell me!'

Ayesha was furiously rummaging under beds, pulling sheets off sleeping children and pushing their tousled heads roughly aside so she could look under the pillows. Maisa started to wail and was quickly silenced by a thump in the guts from a grumpy

Majeeda. Jasmine fell out of bed in the chaos, landing on the floor with a heavy thud. She started to cry. Tamam shouted at his oldest sister that he hadn't got it.

The noise brought Fatima to the foot of the stairs.

'What's going on?!' she screamed. 'Get back in those beds and go to sleep. If I hear any more noise, I'll come up there and beat the lot of you!'

Instantly there was silence and I knew she meant what she said.

Ayesha stood in the middle of the room, still looking for the missing radio. Then she crouched over Tamam and whispered within an inch of his face, 'So if you haven't nicked it, you thieving little sod, who has?'

Tamam smiled. 'Better ask Mum,' he said. 'I think she's got the answer to that.'

Ayesha's face fell. Fatima must've heard her in the kitchen telling us about the radio. 'What am I gonna tell Parveen?' she muttered to no one in particular. 'That was her radio. She lent it me. Mum'll have binned it by now. Parveen's going to kill me.'

'Should've thought of that,' said Tamam. 'Now put the light off, will you?'

Ayesha yanked the cord and we were in darkness again. Tamam wriggled around until he was comfortable, not caring that I was on the receiving end of his feet and elbows.

Finally the room settled down and I dozed off. Tamam, too, relaxed and I could hear snoring from Ayesha's side of the room. The younger girls had also nodded off at last. Until …

'BZZZZ! BZZZZ!! BZZZZ!!! BZZZZ!!!!'

I sat bolt upright, looking round in terror. Something was wrong with the bed. It seemed to be alive, humming and buzzing as though a nest of angry wasps hiding in the mattress had been disturbed. I shook Tamam as hard as I could and tried to clamber over him to get out. In response he pulled himself up, crawled out of bed and pulled the light cord. Everyone woke up. Ayesha chucked a pillow in his direction and pulled her eiderdown over her head. Tamam leaned under the bed and unplugged something. Immediately the noise stopped. Then he pulled at the sheet on top of the mattress and from underneath it yanked out a thick grey blanket with an ominous dark stain spread right across it.

'I piss the bed,' he said simply. 'I do it every night. If you've got a problem with that, lie on the floor. Otherwise shut up.'

I hadn't said a word. Ayesha leaned over and clicked the light off. The mattress was soaked through and I could feel cold pee all over my legs. Horrible, but not so bad if it's your own. If it isn't – disgusting. I turned to the wall and started to cry. Was this what life was going to be like at Aunty Fatima's?

In the days and weeks that followed, I discovered that the answer was 'yes'. 97 Nile Street was cramped, chaotic, often violent (when Fatima delivered the slaps she'd promised on that first night) and always noisy. It's the noise I remember most – the screaming, shouting, bickering, pushing and shoving that inevitably goes on when too many people are packed into a small space. Nile Street was less of a home and more of a crowd, especially when the daily procession of 'aunties' and their children came knocking on the door. True to his word, Tamam pissed the bed every night and mostly slept through the terrible wake-up call of his blanket alarm. Fatima was occasionally woken by it and would come into the bedroom screeching and shouting at us all to get up while she changed the sheets. Every night involved some kind of disturbance. Within a few days I went from a happy, playful child to a withdrawn creature with dark rings around his eyes who craved his own space and spent hours loitering in the alley behind Fatima's backyard.

That said, Tamam wasn't the bully I had him down for on that first night. He turned out to be a nice enough lad, and although he was a couple of years older than me, he didn't resent me being in the house and even seemed to be pleased to have someone to knock around with.

I didn't bother much with the younger girls; they did their own thing and that was fine by me. Ayesha was kind to both Jasmine and me, but seemed to be spending more and more time in the kitchen or sweeping the backyard. There was talk of marriage to a man from Pakistan. Ayesha would go 'home' for the wedding, then come back to live here with her new husband. Her British-born status guaranteed his residency. Was she happy about this? Being so young, I found it hard to know, but I do recall that she would regularly stand on the windowsill in the front bedroom, talking through the unlatched window to other teenagers – boys included – on the street. Sometimes Fatima caught her at it and gave her a big dressing-down in front of the whole family. Talking to boys was 'shameful', she insisted, and was bringing dishonour on their good name around Hawesmill.

'Do you want to get married,' she screeched, 'or are you going to stay on the shelf forever? Because that's the way you're going!'

Ayesha was 15 at the time – stupidly young by Western standards for any talk of marriage, or even engagement. But in Pakistan it wasn't uncommon to find girls half her age in that position. Besides, Yasir was 17 and he was due to get married soon. It was only right that Ayesha should be next.

The front room of the house was Dilawar's little kingdom. He used it as a kind of storeroom for the shop, particularly for valuable and easily-stolen items like cigarettes, and we were never allowed in. Often he would take in his Pakistani news-paper and lock the door behind him, pleased to be away from the noise. He couldn't escape the smell of curry, though, which percolated every room. There was always something bubbling away in a pan on the stove – just as well, given the number of visitors the house received and the odd times of day or night that Dilawar and Yasir would arrive home.

Generally, Dilawar was a kind and quiet man who would only flare up when Tamam was misbehaving. Then he'd beat him severely, leaving the rest of us in no doubt that he would do the same to us if we played up.

One of the highlights of the week was when Dilawar and Yasir came home from the shop with bags full of loose change. They'd pour it all over the low table in the back living room and ask us children to help count it. My cousins were surprisingly good at this, given their age and the fact that attending school wasn't high on the list of priorities in Nile Street. They'd count out piles of coppers and silver, putting them to one side when they'd reached a pound's worth. Yasir or Dilawar would then bag them up, £10 per bag. As far as I could tell, they didn't have a bank account (it's considered un-Islamic to trade with high street banks that have interest rates) and so all the money was kept in the locked front room. That's what passed for family entertainment in that house.

As time went on and Dad's visits became fewer, Fatima took less trouble to disguise her feelings towards us. She'd never been what you might describe as 'warm', but she definitely got worse. She screamed and shouted endlessly and it always seemed to be me who provoked it. Many times she raised her hand, and while she never hit me or Jasmine, the threat was clear. Perhaps she was afraid that we'd tell Dad and she'd get in trouble. Her problem was that she couldn't see us simply as her brother's kids. We also belonged to 'that Englishwoman', the woman who'd entered this close-knit family and taken her brother away. That he'd betrayed his Western wife and taken her kids abroad didn't count; Fatima seemed to believe we were tainted with *kuffar* blood and would always remain outsiders. So why didn't she and the family set us free? The logical decision would've been to return us to our mum. But there was something about this family that made it impossible for them to let go. We would have to stay among them until all traces of Western influence were removed.

But if we were out of sight, we were out of mind. So Fatima created a special punishment for Jasmine and me. If we'd been naughty we were marched upstairs, pushed into the back bedroom and locked in. Occasionally it was both of us, but more often than not, I was alone. I think Fatima knew that Jasmine was young enough to be 're-educated' effectively. She was also female, which carries its own status in Muslim culture. I was a different matter. Perhaps Fatima saw that I would not be so easily moulded. Whatever her reasons, I found myself spending hours in that locked room, staring out over the grey slate rooftops of Hawesmill and wondering what I'd done that was so wrong.

There were times when Jasmine and I clearly hadn't done anything wrong, but were locked in the bedroom anyway. One minute we would be playing with our cousins, the next Fatima would be whisking us upstairs as the whole house erupted in frenzied activity, children and adults running and shouting everywhere. As we were rushed up, I was sometimes certain I could hear the sound of the letterbox flapping at the front door, accompanied by a woman's voice yelling through it. When this happened, the door was never, ever opened, and yet normally a constant stream of visitors walked over that threshold at all times of the day. What was so wrong with this particular visitor that they could not be admitted?

We ourselves weren't allowed out of the house very much. A walk to Dilawar's shop with Fatima or Ayesha was as far as we got. There were no trips to the park, the playground or the seaside. We didn't go into the town. Our whole life was 97 Nile Street and a couple of streets around it. We didn't even go to school. Now I wonder why no school inspectors were on

Fatima's tail, but maybe back then they didn't care whether Asian kids attended or not. However, we were getting an education of sorts at a house at the back of Nile Street that had been knocked through into the house next door and converted into a mosque.

Sebastopol Street was the home of the local imam and his wife. The mosque itself was only for men and older boys, so, with Jasmine, Tamam and Maisa, plus a handful of other little kids from around Hawesmill, I went along several times a week to sit in a side-room and learn the basics of Arabic, making a start on the 114 chapters of the Qu'ran. The imam's wife took the lessons, handing out simple little textbooks which taught the 'ABC' in Arabic, plus other key words and phrases. As we made our first clumsy attempts at this complicated language she listened to us in silence, constantly playing with a set of worry beads. She taught us sentences that form the cornerstones of the Holy Book, for example:

'Bismillāhi r-raḥmāni r-raḥīm
Al ḥamdu lillāhi rabbi l-'ālamīn'

which translates as:

'In the name of God, the most beneficent, the most
merciful,
All appreciation, gratefulness and thankfulness are to
Allah alone, lord of the worlds.'

From an early age all Muslims know these verses from the opening of the Qu'ran, and I was no exception. I'd heard them spoken while in Pakistan. But I found it very difficult to read basic Arabic and also to get the correct pronunciation. The imam's wife would listen to my tongue twisting all over the place and, with an expression like vinegar, hit me with a short stick she kept under the seat. She didn't do it very hard – it was more of a tap than anything else – but it was enough to make me anxious. It also had the opposite effect to that intended: instead of learning to read and speak the verses properly, I became more word-blind and tongue-tied. From that moment on, I struggled with the Qu'ran. It would cause me no end of problems as my childhood progressed.

Chapter Three

After ten months at Fatima's I'd become used to Dad coming and going. He would disappear for weeks on end and although I missed him at first, especially as Fatima obviously had it in for me, his absence wasn't so noticeable day by day. What was becoming annoying was Tamam's constant teasing about my 'white Mum'. It was childish stuff but it hurt, especially when I was locked in the bedroom for retaliating. In there, the same old questions would go round in my mind. Where was she? Did she know we were here? When would she come for us?

The last question was the one I thought about most. As time went on and she didn't appear, I wondered if she'd forgotten us or had found some other kids to be mum to. I must have asked Fatima loads of times about her (and, judging by Tamam's teasing, it was obviously a topic for family discussion when we weren't listening), but she constantly stonewalled me.

In the end, the knock on the door that saved us from a life of punishment and drudgery at Fatima's came not from Mum but from Dad. He appeared one afternoon in late autumn, looking well-fed and satisfied with life. He stepped into 97 Nile Street with a big smile on his face and picked up me and Jasmine in one swoop.

'I'm back, kids,' he shouted, 'and I won't be going away again! I've got us a place to live just round the corner. We're all going home at last.'

We squealed and shouted with happiness. I couldn't believe Dad was back and we were leaving horrible Aunty Fatima's.

We were full of questions, but Dad silenced us with a wave of the hand. 'I know, I know, you want to ask everything,' he said. 'But first I want you to do something. There are some people outside I'd like you to meet. They're in the car. Come on, I'll show you.'

He took us by the hand and led us about 10 yards up the street to an old brown Datsun Sunny. A youngish shy-looking woman in a headscarf sat in the passenger seat, holding a baby. As we got up to the window she stared wide-eyed at us, then up at Dad. In the back of the car were three children who were jumping and scrabbling about like a family of monkeys. They seemed very keen to get out and yet they shrank back from the window as I leaned forward and looked in.

I turned to Dad. 'Who are these people?'

'This,' he said slowly, 'is your new mum. She's come all the way from Pakistan to look after you. Isn't that good?'

'So why's she brought these kids?'

'They're your brother and sisters. We're going to live together. You've got some new kids to play with now, eh?'

Brother and sisters? I didn't get it. Neither could I understand why we needed a new mum. I wanted to ask about the old one, but Dad seemed so happy to see us that I decided not to make him cross by mentioning her. Jasmine and I climbed onto the back seat of the Datsun, squeezing in next to the kids, who had suddenly become strangely silent.

'This is Abida,' Dad said, pointing at the woman in the front seat.

She smiled gently and said, 'Hello there,' in Pashto. I smiled back. She seemed nice – nicer than Fatima anyway.

'And this is Rabida,' Dad continued, gesturing to a girl of about 12. She ignored the introduction and looked out of the window at the row of terrace houses.

'And these little ones are Baasima, Parvaiz and Nahid. Nahid's the baby. Children, this is Mohammed and Jasmine. Say hello, everyone.'

The younger boy and girl, Parvaiz and Baasima, just stared at us. I shuffled around on the leatherette seat, not knowing what to do. The awkward moment was broken by Dad turning the key in the ignition and revving the engine as hard as he could before pulling away up the hill and out of Nile Street. I didn't really care who these strangers were. We'd escaped from Fatima's; for the moment, that was all that mattered.

The car turned into Hamilton Terrace, a street or two away from Fatima's, and stopped outside a house in the middle of the row. From the outside, number 44 looked much the same as 97 Nile Street. The inside was depressingly familiar: two small

rooms and a kitchen downstairs, two little bedrooms and a
bathroom upstairs, plus a yard out the back. What was missing,
thankfully, was Fatima's sour face. I was very pleased about that
and hardly noticed how shabby the house really was. From the
beginning, despite Abida's shyness, this felt like a happy home.

Dad started work as a jobbing builder and handyman, fixing
drains, roof tiles, chimneys and window frames on houses all
over Hawesmill. The condition of the properties meant work
was plentiful. We were glad, not just because it brought some
money in but also because Dad was around a lot more. His trips
to Pakistan stopped and it slowly dawned on me that when Dad
had introduced Rabida, Baasima, Parvaiz and Nahid as our
'brother and sisters' he had been telling us that he was their dad
too. This was the family he'd left behind when he'd journeyed
to England, the family that had patiently waited for him while
he had married Mum and had us two.

Rabida was older than me. The others were younger. Dad
had been a busy man on his trips abroad, that was obvious. I
don't know how Abida had reacted to the news of his English
marriage. I expect she had taken the long-term view that one
day she would come to England and take up her rightful place
as Dad's wife. I don't know how she viewed Mum. Perhaps she
thought she'd share Dad with her, as polygamy is not uncommon among Muslims. Or maybe she knew full well that Mum
wouldn't be around one day.

Dad tried his best to make this flung-together family work.
When he had time off he'd take us all to a nearby park for an
hour or two on the swings. It was lovely for us, because Fatima

had never taken us anywhere. I can see him now, pushing me higher and higher until I could barely breathe with the thrill of it. The more I squealed, the more he laughed, the other kids pulling desperately at his trousers to make sure they got their turn. Once he piled us all into the back of the Datsun Sunny and took us to Blackpool for the day. It must have been my first visit to the seaside. I was overwhelmed by the experience. I sat at the water's edge and dug in the sand, the sea filling up the hole as quickly as I could dig. The beach was packed with holidaymakers and daytrippers, all having fun. Above, seagulls wheeled and cried and I could almost taste the salty wind. It was one of the best days of my life so far and I didn't want it to end.

The sleeping arrangements at Hamilton Terrace were almost as complicated as those at Nile Street, but at least Parvaiz didn't wet the bed. Although there were a lot of us, the atmosphere around the house was nowhere near as frenetic as it had been at Fatima's. Dad treated us all the same, as we were all his children. It was different with Abida: her own children came first every time. If they wanted an apple or a fig, they only had to ask. When Jasmine or I asked, the request was granted, but reluctantly. Now, I see that a mother naturally puts her own first, but back then I just felt that Abida was being difficult and sometimes unfair. At Eid, the holiday that marks the end of Ramadan, little gifts of money or sweets are given to children by adults grateful that the long period of fasting has finished. Abida's four children always filled their pockets with bits and pieces given to them by their mum and dad. Sadly, Jasmine and

I hardly ever shared in their good fortune. Dad, I suppose, was too busy to notice, but we certainly did.

That said, some months after we moved in I asked Abida if I could call her *Ami*, meaning 'Mum'. She seemed very pleased that I thought of her in this way, and from then on I called her Mum at every available opportunity. It was nice to be able to say the word after so long, though it was tinged with sadness because it made me think of my real mum. The old image of the white face and dark hair would flash through my mind and I would desperately try to remember her features. But the memory had long gone.

Finally, I started primary school. I must have been around nine by then and had missed out on a huge amount in terms of reading and writing. There would be a lot of catching up to do, but I was prepared to put the work in.

The school was old-fashioned in terms of the building. The roof leaked in winter and when the boiler packed up in freezing conditions we were always sent home. The teachers were a kindly bunch. They were mainly elderly, female and white, and did their best to educate children who had been born in Britain but whose language and culture were based elsewhere. There weren't many white faces among my classmates. Most white families had moved out of Hawesmill long before, not wanting to live next door to 'Pakis'. Those who did stay put wanted little or nothing to do with us but refused to be 'forced out', as they saw it.

I found white people fascinating. We never went into the town and didn't know any white people, so to be near them in the classroom was very interesting, even if they hardly spoke to me. I wished they would. I would hear Tamam's taunts about the 'white mother' in my head, and wonder what life was like for these kids with white mums and dads. What did they talk about? Where did they go? What did they eat? My curiosity was stirred.

I made some progress at school and still attended the mosque school in Sebastopol Street as well. Abida did her best with us all at home, but she had been raised traditionally and wanted exactly the same for her children. Her girls were all shown how to cook, clean and keep house, and Jasmine was not immune from these chores. I remember coming downstairs one morning to find she'd been up for at least an hour washing the family's clothes by hand in the sink. She was about seven at the time.

Dad seemed happy enough with the domestic arrangements. He breezed in and out of Hamilton Terrace, usually for meals, between labouring jobs. He loved his food, relishing the oily, traditional Pakistani curries made for him by Abida. He would mop up whatever remained with thick pieces of *naan* bread, licking his lips as he swallowed down the last of the rice.

'Mum is a great cook,' he'd say, as she cleared his plate away. 'Best food I've ever had.'

Abida smiled, delighted that she was making her husband happy. After all, there is no greater honour for a Muslim wife than to serve her husband according to the laws of God.

After his meal, Dad would settle back on the settee in the back room, reading his paper and smoking heavily. I very rarely saw him without a cigarette in his mouth, and the house was thick with the smell of tobacco almost all the time, especially when his male friends came round for a chat and a game of cards, just as they would've done back in Tajak.

One of these regular visitors was Rafiq, Abida's brother. A skinny black-bearded man in his forties who always wore the traditional Pathan *topi*, or skullcap, he had left Pakistan some years previously to find work in England and had settled in Bradford with a much younger wife who had eventually walked out on him. They had had no children, so, perhaps out of shame or anger, he had left Bradford and come over the Pennines to Hawesmill. Because he was family, Dad took pity on him and welcomed him into the house. He stayed for a few nights before moving into a shared place around the corner and would come round frequently for food and company. He was a solitary brooding man with a deep voice who certainly wasn't into entertaining us children. We seemed to irritate him hugely and I sensed that given the opportunity, he would lash out. Fortunately Dad was around almost every evening and so Rafiq had little chance to show off the temper I suspected was lurking under the surface.

Dad turned 50 in the early spring of 1985, just before I went into double figures myself. Friends and relations across the north of England were keen to see him, so one afternoon he told Jasmine and me to get our coats. We were going over to Blackburn to pick up a minibus, he explained. Then we'd come back to Hawesmill and collect Abida and the other kids, plus whoever else we could fit in, before heading off to relatives in Bradford. The Yorkshire city had a high number of Pathans living there, and those from the Attock district were either related to or friends of Dad. It would be a big get-together, with plenty of feasting and catching up.

We stood by the old Datsun, pulling impatiently at the passenger door handle. Never mind Bradford, a trip to Blackburn was a big deal, and we couldn't wait to get going.

We waited and waited, and finally I went back into the house to hurry Dad up. I found him sitting in a chair in the front room, wiping his forehead with a handkerchief. Abida was fussing over him. Dad was naturally light-skinned, but he'd turned a weird sickly yellow colour.

I stood by his chair and pulled at his sleeve. 'Come on, Dad, we want to go. Why are you sitting there? Come on, hurry up!'

He turned to me. There were dark rings under his eyes. He was sweating like mad. 'I'm sorry, Moham,' he said, 'I'm not feeling so good. I don't think I'm up to driving.'

I groaned out loud. I really wanted to go. I was sick of looking at the same four walls. I needed a change, even if it was only Blackburn and Bradford.

'Come *on*, Dad,' I pleaded. 'You'll be alright in a minute. We can always stop on the way. *Please*, Dad.'

He didn't reply, just waved his hand in my direction. I sensed someone behind me and looked round. Rafiq was standing there, calmly taking in the scene.

'I'll go and get the minibus,' he said. 'I'll get someone to drive your car back.'

'Thanks, Rafiq,' Dad said, taking a sip of water from a glass. Abida wiped his forehead again. 'Would you mind taking the kids with you? They're desperate for a trip out and I've promised them. Sorry, Rafiq. They'll be good. Won't you?'

I was torn between wanting a trip out and not wanting to go with Rafiq. I knew it would be an uncomfortable journey, but it would be a journey all the same.

'Yes, Dad. I promise.'

'Good lad. Go on then, off you go. I'll be OK by the time you get back.'

I ran out and told Jasmine the news. She scrunched up her face when she heard who was taking us, but luckily she didn't say anything, because within a second Rafiq was out of the front door, car keys in hand. He unlocked the car and indicated that we should get into the back. By trade he was a minicab driver, and we definitely felt like a couple of fares he'd just picked up. Jasmine started chatting straight away, but a look from Rafiq through the rear-view mirror was enough to shut her up and we drove to Blackburn in complete silence.

After 30 minutes or so we arrived at a house in the Whalley Range area of the town. This was the Hawesmill of Blackburn – steep hills, streets full of Asians and not a white face in sight. Like every other in the street, the house we were going to was a small brick-fronted terrace. A gang of kids playing outside peered into the car as we pulled up.

Rafiq let us out, telling us to stand by the car. He went into the house and came out five minutes later with a grey-bearded, grave-looking older man. This man pushed past us and opened the driver's door. He wound down the window, said a quick few words to Rafiq and was gone.

'Follow me,' Rafiq said and we trotted up the hill behind him. Just before the brow of the hill we turned into a scruffy backstreet where a minibus was parked. Again we were consigned to the back seat. Again the journey took place in complete silence. The van smelled of diesel and I hoped I wouldn't be sick. If I was, I knew for sure it wouldn't be Rafiq cleaning it up.

I tried to concentrate on getting home and the journey to Bradford with Dad. We would laugh and joke with him as we crossed the Pennines, pointing out funny things by the road and playing 'I spy'. He'd open the windows and get rid of this horrible fuel smell. Perhaps we'd stop at a café before we reached the city. Once Rafiq was out of the way we'd be fine.

As we reached Hawesmill and pulled into Hamilton Terrace there was a group of people standing outside number 44. Abida was in the middle of a group of women, and I could see Fatima, Ayesha and Yasir, Fatima's eldest son, standing among them.

Rafiq pulled up against the kerb. 'What's going on?' he shouted.

Yasir came over and leaned into the open window. He saw us and silently beckoned Rafiq out. Abida was clutching her *hijab*, or headscarf, across her face. She looked frightened. Someone put a hand on her shoulder and whispered to her. There was something terribly wrong.

The bus's engine was still running as Abida and Rabida got in, along with Yasir. The younger children were hustled back

into the house by Fatima. Rafiq climbed back into the driver's
seat.

'Are we off to Bradford now?' I said. 'Why's Dad not coming?
Is he still poorly?'

Abida took hold of my hand. 'He's not very well,
Mohammed,' she said. 'Not very well at all. He's had to go to
hospital. We're going to see how he is.'

In the front seat Yasir turned round. 'Don't worry, kids,' he
said, smiling. 'He'll be OK. He's just a bit … hurt. We'll see
him soon. That'll cheer him up.'

We parked close by the hospital's A and E department and
hurried through its doors, the adults looking right and left
down the wards to catch a glimpse of Dad. Everyone seemed
to be staring at this scared-looking bunch of foreigners in their
flowing clothes, running down corridors and shouting Dad's
name.

Ahead of us, a man in a white coat saw us coming and put
out his hand to stop us in our tracks. 'Can I help you?' he said
brightly. 'Are you looking for anyone in particular?'

The women looked at one another. They knew no English
and hadn't a clue what the white man in the white coat had
said. Rafiq knew a few words, but not enough to answer the
doctor, and he simply shrugged his shoulders. Fortunately
Yasir's English was good, saving us from looking like a complete
bunch of village idiots.

'We're looking for Ahmed Khan,' he said, 'from Hamilton
Terrace, Hawesmill. He's 50. He's been brought in by ambu-
lance. How is he? Can we see him?'

The doctor looked at his clipboard and ran his finger down a list of names. 'Please, all of you come over here,' he said, 'just to the side of the ward.'

Obediently we shuffled into a small office off the main corridor.

The doctor bit his lip and looked down as he spoke. 'I'm sorry to have to tell you that Mr Khan died half an hour ago. He had a huge heart attack.'

I caught the words but didn't understand. Yasir paused, taking in the terrible news, then translated for Abida and the others. Immediately she started caterwauling, beating her chest and head with her shut fists. Rafiq stared out of the office door, expressionless, as Rabida wept and clung to her mother.

'I'm sorry,' repeated the doctor. 'I'm afraid there was nothing we could do.'

The next hour or so was a blur of tears, screaming, shouting and grief-stricken fury. 'Mr Khan died half an hour ago. Died … died … died …' The doctor's words were repeating in my head. Dad was dead. Something had happened to his heart and he'd died. We wouldn't see him again. He'd gone, this time for good.

This couldn't be happening. I'd never known anyone to die. It seemed a really stupid thing for Dad to do. Stupid enough for him to return home later on, when everyone had stopped crying, and apologize for being so daft. But he wasn't going to. They said he was dead. Dead people didn't come back.

Chapter Four

We arrived at Hamilton Terrace to find the house deserted. Rabida was sent down the street to Fatima's with the bad news. Abida was still weeping and beating her chest. Rafiq and Yasir stood a few feet from her, not wishing to be contaminated by female grief. Muslim men have their own mourning rituals and there is little mutual comfort between the sexes, at least not in public. Jasmine and I stood on the pavement, not knowing where we belonged. Jasmine pulled at the sleeve of Abida's *jilbab*, or coat, but she didn't want to know. She was too caught up in the horrifying shock of what had happened.

Within five minutes Fatima came marching up the street, Rabida behind her, clutching the hands of the little kids we'd left in her care before we set off to the hospital. She was crying hard, but as the nearest of Dad's relatives in this country, she was second in line to the chief mourner and therefore had work to do. The first job was to organize a very large pot of tea and find as many cups as possible.

The men, including Rafiq, Yasir and Dilawar, went into the front room and shut the door. The women trooped into the kitchen with us children. Chairs were arranged in a circle in the back room while Fatima made the tea. She put her arms around Abida and the two cried on each other's shoulders, praying to God for Dad's soul.

News of Dad's death spread quickly and within quarter of an hour the little house was full of people from the surrounding streets. To us, all the women were 'aunty', no matter whether they were related or not. Many of these grieving ladies were gazing at Jasmine and me with pity as we stood bewildered in the back room.

'God bless them,' said one aunty, putting her hand on my head and pulling me to her. 'What have they done to deserve this?'

She squeezed hard and I felt uncomfortable pressed up tight against her *salwar kameez*. As she released her grip, I was bundled into the folds of another mourner, who asked God to forgive us: '*Astaghfirullah.*'

'Don't worry, child,' she whispered in my ear. 'You will be fine. You will be looked after. God has willed it.'

In the far corner of the room Jasmine was getting an equal amount of attention. She was being passed from one aunty to another like a precious china doll. Our step-sisters and brother were around, and just as upset as we were, but getting nowhere near the amount of fuss.

'Oh, Mohammed, God bless you, I'm so sorry about your father. He was a good man.' A tubby aunty stood in front of me, her hand flat on the top of my head. She smiled sympathetically and wiped away a tear. 'God bless you both,' she said, 'you poor little orphans.'

I stepped back, shocked. Orphans? How could we be? I'd heard the word in school, but had taken no notice of it. It seemed to be something that happened to people a hundred years ago. Then I realized: our Dad was dead and our Mum was ... well, where was she? She certainly wasn't here, and we hadn't seen her for seven years. Did that mean she was dead too? Was it something they all knew about, but weren't telling us?

Suddenly I felt very sick, and for the first time that day, my resistance crumbled and I began to cry. This had a chain reaction and soon the tiny back room was filled with women lifting their arms up to God and keening loudly with grief.

Not long after, the front-room door was opened and the men left the house. That room was also full to bursting and they'd decided to find a quieter place. Their way of mourning was to tell old stories about the deceased and make arrangements for the funeral. Under Islamic law the body must be washed, dressed in a shroud and buried as soon as possible, usually within hours of the death. As Dad's body was to be flown back to Pakistan, however, this wasn't possible. His funeral would be in two days, followed by immediate repatriation. In Muslim communities, individuals pay into a fund that covers funeral and travel expenses. One family looks after this money and makes all the arrangements when a person dies. The men were obviously going away to discuss this.

Later that day, Rafiq came back to Hamilton Terrace. This was the signal for the women to leave. With final hugs and kisses, plus pats on the head for us, the aunties went home and another chapter in the life of the Muslim community of Hawesmill was closed. Everything would return to normal once Dad had made his final journey to Pakistan. If only that could be true for me …

A worn-out looking Abida began to wash up all the cups and plates, assisted by Rabida. When the last cup was dried, she turned to us, her eyes puffy and cheeks blotched from crying. 'Go to bed now,' she said. 'Today is a very sad day, but tomorrow will be better. Go on – upstairs.'

She kissed us all one by one and ushered us out of the kitchen. The younger ones clung to her, but she firmly but kindly brushed them off and sent them on their way. She probably wanted time alone to reflect. At 10, I had no concept of that and just wanted someone to hold.

'I don't want to go to bed,' I said. 'I'm frightened. Can I stay down for a bit?'

'No, Moham,' she said, 'not now. It's getting late. Tomorrow we will talk if you want.'

'But *Ami*, I'm scared. Please.'

'*No!*' Rafiq glared at me. 'Upstairs – *now!*'

I stood for a second or two, not knowing whether to stay or go. I could feel him staring at me, waiting for me to make a move. When I did turn towards the stairs it was with deliberately slow movements. I didn't want to disobey him, but neither did I want him to tell me what to do.

I crawled into bed and pulled the covers over my face. Outside, people were still knocking on the door to offer their condolences. Rafiq's deep voice boomed through the thin walls as he thanked people for their thoughts and advised them to come back tomorrow. I thought about the aunty and her 'orphan' reference. Dad wouldn't want me to cry, but I couldn't stop the tears from coming. To know that I wouldn't see his face again was hard enough, but at least he hadn't made the choice to leave us, it had just happened. What about Mum? Had she had a choice? And if she had, why hadn't she chosen to keep us? The same questions went round and round until my mind was playing games with itself and my eyes began to droop …

I woke, or at least I thought I did. Dad was in a corner of the room, looking at me. He seemed to be smiling, reaching out his hand. I stared, blinked … Then he was gone.

I screamed, jumped out of bed and ran downstairs.

'Dad's in my room! *Ami*, Daddy's in my room!'

Abida was sitting in the kitchen, nursing a cup of tea and talking to Rafiq.

'*Ami*, please!' I pulled at her sleeve, wanting her to come upstairs and take away the nightmare I'd just had.

Rafiq was having none of it. He grabbed me by the neck before Abida could stop him and hauled me up the purple-carpeted stairs.

'I've told you once,' he hissed, 'and I won't tell you again. Into bed, go to sleep – or else …'

He pushed me into the bedroom and slammed the door.

I really didn't want to be back in there and immediately turned the light on. The others began to wake up, their tangled little heads rising up sleepily from warm pillows.

Rafiq flung open the door and pushed me hard up against the wall. 'Get to sleep, you bastarrd,' he snarled at me, the 'r' of the last word rolling off his tongue.

'No way!' I screamed. 'I want to come downstairs. I'm scared. I want Abida. I want my dad and my mum. I want them!'

Rafiq let me drop to the floor, walked across the room and turned off the light. Then he came back towards me.

'I warned you, you little bastarrrd,' he said.

He pulled me up again and slapped me as hard as he could across my cheek. The blow knocked the breath right out of me and I slumped against my bed. Then he left the room.

His violence had worked – I was no longer screaming and crying. I was too shocked to react and I sat against my bed for what felt like hours as the force of the blow seeped into my whole body, filling me with fear, shame, embarrassment and anger. I couldn't understand why he'd lashed out like that, but from that moment onwards I knew that nothing in my life would ever be the same again.

I slept under the bed that night, terrified that I might see Dad again and scream, making Rafiq come tearing up the stairs again.

Early in the morning I sneaked downstairs and into the kitchen for a glass of water, hoping not to wake anyone.

'Hey, you … bastarrd,' a deep, guttural voice called from the front room as I passed.

Rafiq had obviously slept on the settee. I said a quick prayer to God that I'd not woken him up.

'In here,' he said, beckoning me to the side of the settee with his index finger.

Terrified, I obeyed him.

'What was all that howling for last night?' he said. 'You better start growing up, boy, and fast. Because I'm in charge now.'

I asked him what he meant.

He laughed. 'Wait and see, boy,' he said, 'wait and see.'

I backed away from him, a nauseous feeling crawling through my stomach. He watched me like a snake watches a mouse. Then he pointed at me.

'Be very careful, bastarrd,' he said. 'I'm waiting for you.'

By 9 a.m. everyone was up, but still dazed from the terrible events of the previous day. Far from being the centre of attention, Jasmine and I were now left to our own devices as more aunties came round to help and the men went to the mosque at the top of Hawesmill to wash Dad's body, which had just been delivered there by the undertaker. This is an important ritual in Islam. The body must be purified before burial and the male relatives of the deceased will wash it before wrapping it in a shroud. I was told I wasn't allowed to go with them, because I was too young. I wasn't sorry; I imagined the men lifting Dad up to wash him at a sink, his head flopping forward and his legs buckling under him as they applied a flannel to his face. The thought horrified me.

Abida spent most of the day in the kitchen, attended by female visitors, while Fatima bustled about, cooking samosas and making tea. Like many Muslim families, we didn't have an electric kettle. The preferred method was to set a large pan of water to boil on the stove, into which were placed tea bags, plenty of sugar and milk. Once this was ready, it would be transferred to a teapot.

We were sent out to play in the alley behind the house. Jasmine was very subdued and kept going back inside to hang around with the women. I stayed outside, kicking a saggy football against a nearby back gate until the owner of the house came out and gave me a bollocking. When he realized who I was, he stopped shouting and blessed me instead. Then he told me to bugger off.

For hours I wandered around the dusty pothole-riddled backstreets around Hamilton Terrace, trying to picture all the people who'd lived around here before me. We'd done a bit about it in school. Our teacher had showed us old photos of white kids without shoes, their faces all dirty. The men and the women all looked the same: same clothes, same flat caps, same headscarves. They looked tired and fed up. They looked like the people living around Hawesmill now, except a different colour. Nothing nice ever seemed to happen around here. No parties, games, music, fun, laughter. The evening shadows were lengthening across the slated roofs. I couldn't put off the dreaded moment any longer and lifted the rusty latch that led into the backyard of number 44.

Through the kitchen window I could see Abida and Fatima. The door was slightly open and as I walked up I could hear them talking.

'Oh, Fatima,' Abida wailed, 'what's to be done? Ahmed had no money, nothing put by for a rainy day. And all these children around. What will I feed them with? I don't know where to begin, I really don't.'

I moved closer to the door and saw Fatima touch Abida's arm.

'Then you should do what Rafiq suggests,' she said, 'and let him move in. It makes sense and it is not unfitting. It is the right thing.'

'But he's no good with the children,' Abida said. 'They irritate him.'

'He will learn,' Fatima replied, 'and I hope he will be strict. My brother was far too soft. They need bringing into line. Especially you-know-who …'

At that moment I walked in. 'Hello, aunty,' I said, as brightly as possible.

Caught in the act, Fatima looked away for a moment. 'Ah, Mohammed,' she said, 'and where've you been?'

'Out playing.'

'Playing?! And your father's dead just one day. How irreverent. I hope you'll be attending mosque for prayers this evening. Go upstairs and wash.'

'Don't bother him, Fatima,' Abida whispered quickly, 'he's still in shock. They're all wandering about like lost lambs.'

'Oh come on, Abida,' Fatima snapped, 'the boy's 10. He should be acting like the man of the house, not some urchin in the street. Go on, Mohammed, get washed!'

Abida went quiet, deferring to her elder. I slunk past them both and went upstairs to the bathroom. Reluctantly I washed myself and changed my jumper for a clean one. I hardly had any clothes and I was trying to save this top for the funeral. But if I went to mosque in my dirty one, someone would notice and it would get back to Fatima or Abida. Or worse still, Rafiq. I remembered his boast about 'being in charge' and Fatima talking about him moving in. I couldn't think of anything worse.

Ten minutes later I left the house and began the walk round the corner to the mosque in Sebastopol Street. I was still annoyed at Fatima telling me off just for playing football and at Abida for chickening out of standing up for me. It wasn't fair that I'd been shouted at, especially when my Dad had just died. And I was going to mosque anyway – I didn't need to be reminded. Since I'd got into double figures I'd been attending regularly, which I was obliged to do, and I hardly ever missed it. Why did Fatima seem to suggest that I was trying to get out of it? In a temper I kicked a stone across the street, narrowly missing the door of a parked Fiesta.

Then I had a thought – why should I bother going tonight? I would be going to Dad's funeral the next day. No one would miss me, and even if they did, I was sure I wouldn't be shouted at, not when my Dad was lying in his coffin. Instead of carrying on down Sebastopol Street I turned off into Argyle Street and sneaked into the 'backs'. By now it was dark. If I hung around here for an hour, I wouldn't be spotted.

From the dark of the alleyway I could see men and boys going to evening prayers, illuminated by the street lamps. Hundreds of people literally squeezed into the two terrace houses which formed the mosque. In that kind of a crush I surely wouldn't be missed.

Shivering, I paced up and down the backs until I saw the first trickle of people returning the same way they'd come. Unnoticed, I slipped out of the darkness and mingled with the worshippers going home. I recognized a few faces under *topi* hats, but no one spoke to me and I was alone again when I turned into Hamilton Terrace.

Abida greeted me as I came through the door and asked me if I wanted something to eat. Standing around in the chill of an autumn evening had made me very hungry, and I eagerly accepted a plate of curry and a rolled-up chapati. I'd almost finished when the lock was turned in the front door. For a moment I thought it was Dad and jumped up to greet him. Then I remembered ...

'Ah, there you are, Mohammed.'

It was Rafiq, standing in the doorway of the living room, staring at me in an odd way and smiling.

'Did you enjoy mosque tonight?' he said.

'It was alright,' I mumbled through a mouthful of curry.

'So ... did you find what the imam said interesting?'

'Er, yeah. Did you?' Nervously I looked away. The feeling I'd had the previous night returned to the pit of my stomach.

'I did,' he said. 'Which part did you find the most interesting?'

He was still smiling. He was enjoying this.

'Umm, probably the bit about … being good … and going to heaven? I enjoyed that.'

'Excellent!' Rafiq leaned over and patted me on the back like an old friend. 'I'm so pleased to hear you're paying attention. But … were you at a different mosque tonight, Mohammed?'

'No. Why?' I could feel beads of sweat on my forehead, and the back of my neck was hot.

'Only because Imam Farouk wasn't very well tonight, as he said, and didn't deliver the *khutbah*. So I'm not sure who you were listening to, Mohammed. Or if you were even there at all …?'

Rafiq moved from the doorway and sat uncomfortably close to me on the settee. He put his mouth right up to my ear.

'Put down your food, go upstairs and wait for me,' he hissed.

I dared not disobey him. I left the half-eaten bowl of curry on the arm of the settee and walked upstairs as calmly as I could, though I thought my legs would collapse on me at any moment.

The younger children were already asleep. I sat on the edge of my bed, my hands on my lap and my head bowed. Tomorrow was Dad's funeral. None of this should be happening.

Rafiq let me sweat for 10 minutes before strolling up the stairs. He seemed to be in no rush.

Again he sat too close to me. 'You didn't go to mosque tonight, did you, Mohammed?'

I shook my head in response.

He tutted. 'That was wrong, very wrong. You know what the Holy Prophet, peace be on him, says about going to mosque?'

'As a Muslim I am obliged to go to mosque,' I mumbled.

'That's right. So why didn't you go?'

'I did! I was … squashed in at the back. I left early because I couldn't hear very well. I thought Imam Farouk was speaking, but maybe he wasn't, I think it was someone else, I definitely heard those words, I …'

I was waffling, and he knew it. Suddenly he grabbed me by the neck and shoved me against the wall, just as he'd done the night before.

'I warned you, you bastarrrrd!' he said, raising his hand. I knew I was going to get it, but I wasn't going down without a fight. I tried to wrestle out of his grip, kicking and twisting to get away.

'Get off me!' I screamed. 'You're not my dad!'

Immediately he relaxed his grip. I leaned against the wall, breathing heavily.

'You're right, Mohammed,' he said, his face twisted into a mask of hate, 'I'm not.'

And with that he raised his shut fist and punched me full in the nose. I heard a delicate bone crack on impact and I went straight down on the carpet. Blood was gushing over my mouth and onto my clean jumper. I tried wiping my nose, but it was too painful, and the sight of thick blood oozing across my palm made me feel sick.

Rafiq stood over me as I squirmed in agony. I looked up at him, my face a mixture of tears, blood and snot. He said nothing, just turned on his heel and left the room as calmly as he'd entered.

Surprisingly, none of the kids sharing the bedroom had been woken up by the violence – or if they had, they'd put their heads under the covers and kept very, very quiet. I don't know how I got to sleep, with a face that felt as though it had been rammed against a brick wall, but somehow I did.

The pain was still there the following morning, and when Jasmine woke up and saw me, she screamed in horror. I shushed her up, explaining that I'd fallen off a wall while playing out and that I was OK. Today was Dad's funeral. I didn't want to give her any reason to be more upset than she already would be.

With hindsight, I should've gone straight down and told Abida what Rafiq had done. But I wasn't sure that she'd believe me over her own brother. After all, I was the son of her rival for Dad's affections, the spawn of the woman Dad had cheated on her with. She was as nice as she could be to me, but I didn't know if I could trust her. And when Fatima had spoken about 'you-know-who' to her, I'd just known she was referring to me. Maybe Abida also believed I was bad. So I chose to say nothing, and when I came downstairs to breakfast with Abida, Rafiq and the children, nothing was said. It was as if I'd woken up with a slight sniffle.

Dad's funeral was at the mosque, of course. According to custom, women stayed at home, so I accompanied Rafiq, Yasir and Dilawar to the service. The imam stood at the front and began to recite the funeral prayer, the 'Salat al-Janazah'. This was accompanied by a lot of hand-raising and touching of the chest and various periods of kneeling and prostrating on the floor of the mosque. I'd never been to a funeral before and could barely understand what was going on, so I just attempted to copy everyone else.

Then the time came to ceremonially walk around the open coffin. I was nervous, as I had no wish to see my dad looking, well, *dead*, but Yasir steered me forward and I peeped over the top of the open box. Dad looked peaceful; tired, but peaceful. In a way, seeing him dead wasn't such a bad thing, for now I knew that he had gone and wasn't coming back.

Uncles and cousins patted me on the head and shook my hand after my walk around Dad's body, telling me what a brave boy I was for not crying. The truth was somewhat different. I'd desperately wanted to cry, but as soon as I'd started to sniffle the pain in my nose had become unbearable and I'd had to stop. To make matters worse, Rafiq was playing the concerned relative, taking me to people who wanted to offer their condolences and agreeing that I was bearing up remarkably well. I could've punched him in the balls for what he'd done to me, but his powers of manipulation were too strong.

Finally, the imam said the words *'Assalaamu 'alaykum wa rahmatu-Allah wa barakatoh'* ('Accept my thanks and gratitude, and may Allah bless you and direct your path') and we left the mosque. Dad's body would be taken by hearse to Heathrow airport then depart for Pakistan in a few hours. Two of his older relatives went with it.

I was escorted home and arrived to find, once again, a kitchen full of wailing women. It was all too much, so I sat in the backyard, scratching patterns on the moss-covered flag-stones with a broken piece of slate. In the living room Rafiq was making himself comfortable on Dad's favourite side of the settee, settling down with a newspaper and looking extremely pleased with himself.

Chapter Five

In Dad's absence Rafiq appeared to make himself useful, at least in the first few months. He brought in some money – though never quite enough – as a taxi driver and would regularly do the shopping, arriving home with meat and vegetables for that evening's tea. He even spent time talking to us children about our day and playing a little cricket or football with us in the backstreet. But his new-found parenting skills did not extend my way. He rarely spoke to me, and when he did, it was to interrogate me on what I was doing.

Abida seemed happy with her brother being around and chose to ignore his brutality on the night before Dad's funeral. I think she was just pleased not to be alone; in her eyes Rafiq was providing for her and looking after the children. That was more than enough from a Pakistani man.

From an early age I'd worn mainly Western clothes, a mixture of hand-me-down or jumble-sale jeans, jumpers, shirts and cheap trainers thrown together with bits and pieces from traditional Muslim dress – *salwar kameez* tops and *topi* hats.

Most kids my age were the same, and very few people thought it wrong or 'un-Islamic'. We were all poor, and what we wore was a reflection of how much our parents had in their pockets. But Rafiq was different. Although he was personally happy to wear shirts, jeans and trainers while out working, he decided that I would be forbidden from wearing the *gora*, a term used to refer to white people. In this case he meant the English way of dressing. Even though I usually wore my jeans underneath my *salwar kameez*, they had to go, along with all my T-shirts. Rafiq gave no reason for this, except that he didn't like seeing me in English clothes. I was allowed to keep my trainers only because they were black, and proper leather shoes were expensive.

Then there was the ongoing mosque issue. Rafiq pinned a calendar on the kitchen wall which gave the five different prayer times each day. There would be no more excuses; I would go to mosque five times a day, each and every day, and he would monitor my movements very closely.

After the beating I'd had from him I dared not disobey. It was a struggle getting up for dawn prayers, but I made sure I stuck to the timetable. Gradually I learned the ways of the mosque, like how to carry out the *wudu* ablutions, or purification rituals, before prayer. The Hawesmill mosque, like all mosques large or small, was fitted with a long metal trough with cold-water taps above it. Every time you go to pray, you have to wash yourself in a certain sequence – usually hands, mouth, nostrils, face, right and left arms, ears, neck and feet. After this you go into the prayer hall and line up in rows facing

Mecca. There are prayers and readings from the Qur'an, plus religious or cultural speeches on being a good Muslim. The mosque has a strict hierarchy: elders at the front, their sons behind and boys at the back. Of course, all the prayers and readings from the Qur'an are in Arabic. Some Muslims pick this up very easily; I always struggled and although I was eventually able to repeat phrases parrot-fashion, it was almost impossible for me to understand what they meant. Having no one to guide me, I fell far behind in this respect.

All the time the beady eye of Rafiq was on me. I would carefully watch for the signal to kneel down or stand up again, knowing that he was waiting for me to slip up. Sometimes I did, and the result would be a blow to the back of the head as we walked home or, later on, a hammering in the confines of the bedroom. As he was doing it, he would mutter to himself. I heard him repeating the same words around the house during the day and realized he was reciting verses from the Qur'an. I assume he was justifying to himself the beatings he was handing out.

I remained as dutiful as I could, but sometimes it wasn't easy. One night, just after I'd turned 11, I was coming home from evening prayers alone. To reach the mosque you had to go through a subway which went under the main road that cut Hawesmill in two. I'd never liked this tunnel. Rainwater, waste oil and urine mixed to form grim pools across its concrete floor and most of its orange lights had long since gone out. It was full of graffiti and a magnet for glue-sniffers from across the area. That night, as I picked my way carefully through the puddles in my cheap trainers, I noticed a couple of kids lurking near the exit.

It was too late to walk back. I went forward, my head held as high as possible. 'I'm not scared, I'm not scared,' I said to myself, hoping the mantra would protect me. But as I approached, I could see these kids were a year or two older than me – a lifetime when you're that age.

'Ey, look what's coming,' said one of them, 'a little Paki! Awreet, curry breath, where are you going then?'

I tried not to look at the two white lads who were now standing in front of me, blocking the way out of this filthy place. I recognized one of them, a well-known troublemaker nicknamed Boo-Boo who lived in the mainly white estate beyond Hawesmill but ventured round our way whenever he dared.

'Where've *you* been?' he said aggressively, pushing me in the chest as he spoke.

'I've just been to mosque … to church, you know? I'm going home now. Can I go past?'

'No, you fucking can't. Not until you say "Please, sir".'

'Look, I just want to get home,' I said, trying not to shake. 'My mum and dad are waiting for me. They'll be mad if I'm late.'

As soon as the lie came out of my mouth I realized how truly alone I was. Strangely, it made me feel stronger. Whatever these two bullies were planning to do, it wouldn't be anywhere near as bad as what was waiting for me at home.

'Say "Please, sir",' Boo-Boo repeated.

'Piss off,' I replied and shoved past him as hard as I could.

I started to run, but he grabbed my coat sleeve and swung me round, punching me in the eye. His mate laughed and tried to swing a kick in my direction, but missed and overbalanced, falling to the ground. Boo-Boo hesitated for a second, thinking that I'd somehow tripped his mate, and I took advantage by pulling away and running off. They didn't bother to chase me – in an Asian area they'd have stood out like two white sore thumbs, and Hawesmill certainly wasn't short of lads who were handy with their fists.

I went into the house via the back door and ran straight upstairs to the bathroom, locking the door. An old sock was half-hanging out of the wash basket. I ran it under the tap and dabbed my swollen eye with it. When I was finished I opened the door, checked the coast was clear and went straight to bed.

That night I lay awake, thinking about the attack in the subway, Rafiq's petty cruelties and his nit-picking attitude. I wondered why the family wouldn't just let me go home to Mum. I thought about this a lot. If they couldn't stand me, surely it would've been better for them to hand Jasmine and me back? That was, if Mum was still around, of course, or even still alive. I had no idea about either possibility. Her name was still occasionally mentioned when Abida or Rafiq or Fatima thought I wasn't listening, accompanied by tutting and shaking of the head.

There was also still the odd time that a knock at the door remained unanswered. Once, as I was coming downstairs, there was a knock on the door and I was the nearest person to it. I had a feeling that behind it would be a woman with long dark hair and a big smile. Before anyone else could get to it, I flung it open. I was right. The woman on the doorstep had long dark hair and a big smile – but she was Asian. Just another 'aunty' from up the street, calling round for a cup of tea and a chat.

The next day I was woken up as usual by Rafiq roughly pushing me and demanding I get up for mosque. I complied, knowing that Boo-Boo and his mate would still be in bed. But as the day went on I became more fearful of meeting the pair again. When it came time for evening prayers I decided to appeal to Rafiq's better nature.

'You what, bastarrd?' he said, as he slouched in Dad's old seat, legs splayed out. 'Tell me again – you don't want to go to mosque tonight?'

'You don't understand,' I pleaded. 'There were these two lads, white lads. They beat us up under the subway. Look at my eye!'

He grabbed me by the arm and pulled me towards him, poking my painful and swollen eyelid.

'That's nothing compared to what I'll give you if you don't go!'

'Please, Uncle Rafiq, I'm scared. Will you come with me then?'

'What are you scared of?' he snapped. 'You said they were white boys. So tell them you're a white boy too, *kuffar*!'

With that, he grabbed me and pulled me out of the living room. 'Here we go again,' I thought. But he didn't go upstairs. Instead he pushed me down the hallway, through the kitchen and into the backyard. In one corner there was an outside toilet, left intact from Victorian days. It still worked, and was occasionally used when the bathroom was occupied. I hated going in there. It was dark, smelly and full of spiders. Rafiq knew I didn't like it, and without further ado he pushed me in and locked the door from the outside.

'That's where pigs belong,' he said, walking back into the house.

I kicked the bottom of the door and yelled, but it made no difference. Rafiq had shut the kitchen door and no one could hear me. I groped for the toilet seat, pulled it down and sat on it, keeping as still as a statue in the hope that I wouldn't disturb the spiders' webs hanging in sinister drapes above my head.

After an hour or so I heard footsteps in the yard. The bolt was pulled back. Then the latch was lifted and the door swung open.

'Out you come, bastarrd,' Rafiq said. 'I hope you've learned your lesson. Tell me again – what are you doing this evening?'

'Going to mosque, Uncle Rafiq.'

'Good. Now get gone. And if I hear any more from you, that toilet will be your bedroom for the night.'

I did as I was told.

I didn't see Boo-Boo or his sniggering mate round the subway again, and if I had, I think I would've transferred Rafiq's bullying onto them, and given as good as I got. I wasn't big or strong for my age, but I'd have gone down fighting. Perhaps that's what should have happened, for what was to come made my life far more difficult than I could ever have imagined.

* * *

There were plenty of other boys my age going to mosque and in the days after the attack in the subway I latched onto a group of them – safety in numbers and all that. They were Pathans, all around my age. I enjoyed their easy banter and stupid jokes. To me, they seemed very worldly and confident. Most of them were at school too, a privilege that I hadn't been allowed to enjoy much so far. Dad's death had put paid to my schooling; one minute I was there, the next I wasn't. As far as I know no one from social services ever came round asking questions about my non-attendance. If they did, they must've been fobbed off somehow. I've never really got to the bottom of this and can only assume that among Rafiq's long list of prejudices against the society that kept him housed and fed was a hatred of 'English' schools. To him, the only knowledge you needed came from mosque, and from then on that would be my sole place of education.

Haani and Sadeeq were the leaders of the mosque-going pack. They were two years older than me and would smoke cigarettes on the way home from mosque in that hide-it-from-Mum, cupped-hand teenage style. They swapped dirty jokes and made remarks about local girls. I thought they were funny and daring; they were a world away from Rafiq's oppressive regime and soon I began to hero-worship them. They treated me like a little brother. I suppose I was the runt of the pack, being the smallest and youngest, but I became a kind of mascot and they seemed to enjoy the fact that I looked up to them, star-struck.

One evening Sadeeq declared that he was bored with school. 'I'm skiving off tomorrow and the next day,' he said, 'and

I know a place we can go.' He nudged Haani knowingly. 'Who's coming?'

The two or three other boys who made up this little pack shook their heads. They knew what would happen if their dads caught them. Not every Asian family in Hawesmill had the same attitude to education as Rafiq. There were plenty who wanted to see their children get on in the West and make something of themselves. After all, that's why they were here. Sadeeq and Haani understood this, but they still teased the 'softies' who wouldn't skip school for a day or so's fun.

Not wanting to miss out or upset my new friends, I eagerly volunteered to go along to wherever they were going. Skiving school wasn't an issue; as long as I didn't miss mosque, I would be fine.

The following day I met Haani and Sadeeq at the corner where Sebastopol Street met Alma Street. We walked down the broad sweep of Alma Street, right to the very bottom of Hawesmill.

'Where are we going, lads?' I said, almost skipping by their sides.

'Got a big surprise for you, Moham,' said Haani, tugging on the dark adolescent fuzz above his top lip that he laughingly called 'a tache'. 'You won't never have seen nothin' like this before, I tell ya!'

Sadeeq grinned and grabbed my shoulder. 'Your eyes will be opened, little brother,' he said, 'your eyes will be opened.'

I laughed nervously. These two were rascals, I knew, but what had they got planned that would 'open my eyes'? I was so naïve that I didn't even know what that phrase meant.

'In here,' said Haani, indicating a house tucked away in a terrace row of about five or six identical properties. He pushed open a front door that was worn-looking and striped with cracked green paint, and led us into the back room.

Instinctively I shrank bank when I saw what was waiting for us there. Sprawled across an old brown and orange velour settee were three girls, all aged about 15. They were all heavily made up and sported loose curly perms. The shocking pastel pinks, greens and blues of their tight-fitting tops and skirts were in sharp contrast to the squalid surroundings of this terrace house. There were glimpses of cleavage and flashes of thigh. Two of them were smoking and giggling, while the other one was nonchalantly chewing gum and flicking through that week's copy of *Smash Hits*. For an 11-year-old boy raised entirely within Islam, it was shocking stuff. But what shocked me even more was the fact that they were white. Except for a brief period at school I had never been this close to white girls before, and certainly not white teenage girls whose hormones appeared to be bursting out in every direction.

'Your eyes will be opened.' Sadeeq wasn't joking. I stared, unblinking, for what felt like a full 10 minutes, my mouth gaping like a stranded fish.

Meanwhile Haani was rummaging for his fags, while Sadeeq was rattling through a pile of cassette tapes stacked next to a cheap ghetto blaster on the windowsill, looking for something more moody. The girls did their best to ignore us, but this meeting was no coincidence. Somehow Sadeeq and Haani had persuaded them to cross the invisible racial border into

Hawesmill and join them for a day of skiving ... and whatever else. Questions raced through my mind. How had my Asian mates met them? What had they said to get them to come here? What was going to happen now?

'Who's he?' said the gum-chewer, tossing her dark curls in my direction. 'Oi, lad ... what the fuck are you starin' at?'

'Nothing,' I said, casting my eyes to the ground as I'd been taught to do whenever a woman passed me on the street.

'Jesus, look at him, he's going red!' she said. 'He's a Paki and he's going red! Is he your lickle brother or summat?'

'Don't call him a Paki,' said a defensive Haani. 'He's not our brother. Not in that way. He's a mate, aren't you, Moham? He just wants to come and have a laugh with us.'

The girl softened. 'Awwww, I'm sorry for teasing you, love,' she said. 'I were only takin' the mick. Come on, sit down. What's your name? I'm Debbie and this is Jane and Carol.'

'Hiya,' the other two chorused, looking totally bored.

I sat down by Debbie, inching as far away as I could without her noticing. Which she did, of course.

'What's up wi' me?' she said. 'Do I stink or summat? Least I don't smell of curry ...'

'Oi!' I said. 'That's racist, that.'

She laughed, and I laughed too. 'I'm teasing again,' she said. 'You'll get used to me.'

'I dunno,' I replied. 'I might not be coming again.'

'Why not? We come every day, don't we, lads?'

Haani and Sadeeq nodded in agreement. So they'd been bunking off school for ages, and this is where they'd hidden out.

Jane and Carol were now chatting and flirting with my friends as though they'd known each other ages; I wondered what the parents of these white girls would think if they knew they were here. A mental picture of Rafiq's face suddenly appearing at the window flashed into my mind, and I shuddered. I knew exactly what he would do if he caught me ...

The day passed quickly, and in my fascination I forgot totally about mosque. I was shy and hesitant that first time, only speaking when I was spoken to and definitely not accepting offers of cigarettes from Haani and Sadeeq. I felt guilty enough listening to *Now That's What I Call Music* on the cassette player. Rafiq hated hearing Western pop songs around the house and made every effort to ban them. If there was a glimpse of *Top of the Pops* on the television it would almost cause a meltdown. I was always to blame, probably because I was half-white and therefore had the 'devil's music' inside me. Even so, I occasionally sneaked upstairs and listened to the transistor radio Ayesha had given me just before she got married. My favourite song was Tiffany's 'I Think We're Alone Now'. I was at the age when I could imagine myself with Tiffany 'alone now' in a bedroom in Hawesmill. Thinking about white girls was wrong, I knew; even so, I couldn't help feeling those same feelings now, confronted by Lancashire's answer to Tiffany – or maybe Bananarama – in this dingy terrace house at the bottom of the hill.

After about four hours we left, agreeing to meet Debbie, Jane and Carol again in a few days' time. I could hardly wait. I was unable to articulate the excitement and anticipation I felt.

The girls had been a bit flirty and giggly, but there seemed to be nothing more on offer than that. Haani and Sadeeq certainly weren't boasting of any sexual conquests with the trio and I got the impression the little out-of-school liaison was nothing more than a bit of fun. I dreaded Rafiq finding out, but as I wasn't going to school anyway, hopefully he wouldn't ask too many awkward questions.

One thing nagged me, though – the fact that I would burn in hell. If Rafiq didn't know where I was, Allah certainly did. We'd had a couple of preachers at the mosque who'd mentioned the consequences of associating with white people and adopting their wicked ways. I'd taken notice of this, for obvious reasons, and now the idea of eternal fires was tormenting me at night. I prayed to Allah for forgiveness and hoped He wouldn't punish me too severely. I even toyed with making a solemn promise not to visit the old house again, but every time I came near the vow I backed off; in my heart I knew I was very drawn to the white girls and what they represented, and I didn't dare make a promise I knew I would break.

Four days after the first meeting I slipped out of the house once again and met Haani and Sadeeq at the corner of Sebastopol and Alma. It was a warm and sunny morning, and my mood reflected the weather. We were going to have a great day hanging out with the girls, listening to music and chatting. I decided I might even try a cigarette. My mates looked sort of cool when they smoked. My dad had smoked too, so it must be OK. Though of course he was dead, the victim of a smoking-related heart attack. I pushed that thought from my mind and joined in Haani and Sadeeq's banter as they swaggered down the street, seemingly careless about who saw them out on a school morning.

Debbie, Jane and Carol were waiting. Haani had told me the house belonged to a friend of his dad's. This man had bought it with the idea of doing it up and had asked Haani's dad to look after the key while he visited Pakistan. That had been more than a year before and Haani reasoned that if he wasn't coming back, he might as well put it to some use. I wondered how many people had a copy of that key, but despite its shabbiness, the house was well kept and Haani always made us tidy up before we left. In a weird teenage way he was quite house-proud.

'So, what've you been doing, Moham?'

Debbie was all done out in a pink sleeveless vest, white pedal-pushers and pastel lipstick. She looked like Sheena Easton, whose posters I'd seen pasted onto walls during fleeting visits outside Hawesmill. I was curious about Debbie; I imagined that if things had turned out differently I might have lived next door to her. She'd have been my childhood friend who one day became my wife.

'Nothing much,' I said. 'Just dossing about, going to mosque, you know?'

'I wouldn't go to a mosque,' she replied. 'Anyway, they wouldn't let me in.' Then she paused. 'Can I ask you summat personal?'

My cheeks flushed. I couldn't imagine what she would ask, or how embarrassed I'd be.

'What is it?'

She took a breath. 'How come you're a Pakistani but you're ... dead white looking? I'm not being funny, but I thought all Pakis were brown. Why aren't you?'

I could see Jane and Carol looking at me intently. They'd obviously been discussing this in the days since we'd last met them.

I coughed and shuffled awkwardly on the settee. 'It's 'cos I'm a Pathan,' I said.

'What's a pattern?' said Carol gormlessly.

I explained that my dad was from north-west Pakistan and that the tribes up there were paler-skinned than in the rest of the country.

Haani and Sadeeq sniggered.

'It's not the whole truth, though, is it?' said Haani, looking at me expectantly. He knew I was too shown up to say anymore.

'Moham looks white because he is,' he added.

'No, I'm not!'

'You are! OK, you're half-white. His mum's white. Inn't she, Moham? Go on, tell 'em.'

'My mum's white,' I repeated. 'She's from Manchester. But I dunno where she is now.'

'No way!' said Debbie, open-mouthed. 'Is she a Muslim? How come she ended up marrying one? I thought that were illegal. God ... I dunno if I could marry one. No offence, lads.'

I explained that my mum had met my dad at work but they'd split up and we'd gone to Pakistan. Trying to tell them who I was living with now was complicated, so I gave up and steered the conversation elsewhere.

Debbie, however, wouldn't give up and kept asking me questions about my mum and how I felt about her. No one had ever talked to me like this before. I couldn't believe how open and frank she was with me. Tentatively I threw a few questions back – where did she live, what did her parents do, what was being English like? I desperately wanted to hear everything, even down to why she thought that a bacon butty was the most delicious food ever.

'It's disgusting,' I said. 'It's unclean. Pigs are dead dirty.'

'Who said that?!' she laughed. 'What a load of crap. You should have one – you never know until you try. My dad has bacon, sausage and black pudding all on one butty, covered in HP sauce. A pig sandwich!'

I'd never heard of black pudding, so Debbie filled me in. I shuddered inwardly and said it sounded horrible.

Debbie said she'd never eaten curry in her life and never would. 'It stinks,' she said. 'Ugghhh!'

We bantered like this for ages. It was childish stuff, but I loved hearing things about English life. The way Debbie described her family's lives made them sound like creatures from another world. All the things they had, everything they did, talked about, visited, ate – everything was completely different from my world and yet Debbie and I lived less than a mile apart. How could that be?

We were still chatting when Haani lifted his finger up, looking at us wildly.

'Shurrup!' he whispered. 'I thought I heard something …!'

We sat as still as statues. There it was again, the unmistakable flap of the letterbox. There was someone on the other side of the door! It couldn't be the postman. Then there came the heavy stomach-churning sound of a big fist banging on the wood, accompanied by a shout.

'Mohammed! Are you in there? Come out now!' A deep guttural Pashto speaker was outside.

Then came the sound of talking – there were other people out there.

'Kick the door down,' one said. 'It's empty anyway. The council will fix it back up.'

Inside, the three girls shook with fear. Carol began to cry. Haani ran to the back door and bolted it. This was supposed to be a laugh, a doss, a bit of fun. Suddenly it had turned into a terrible nightmare.

'Fuck! What are we gonna do?!' Sadeeq was almost white with terror.

Fists thudded on the door over and over again.

'Mohammed Khan! *Get out now!*'

'Upstairs,' Haani ordered, 'and find somewhere to hide! We'll keep them at the door. They're after you, not us. Go on. Run!'

I tore up the stairs, two at a time, as the hammering intensified. There was nothing in either bedroom, not a bed, wardrobe or chair. Nowhere to hide.

Downstairs, Haani cleared his throat and opened the door. I heard him yelp as it was shoved forwards into his face and heavy footsteps pounded upstairs.

I looked round. There was an old-fashioned sash window, half open, with a rusty drainpipe just close enough to the windowsill. I didn't know what would be worse, a fall from the bedroom window or the terrible beating I would get in five seconds flat.

Sweating with terror, I shoved up the sash and crawled through the window.

Chapter Six

I was about 15 feet up, but it felt like 50. Trying not to panic, I swung out and anchored my feet either side of a thick joint around the rusty drainpipe. By the look of it, the drainpipe had been put in when the house had been built a hundred years ago. I had no idea how – or if – it would hold a growing lad, but I was about to find out.

Almost crying with fear, I inched carefully down the pipe below the level of the windowsill. Just above, there were shouts from the bedroom, then a face leaned out of the open sash.

'Where d'you think you're going, you little fucker?!'

It was Yasir, Aunty Fatima's eldest son. His head darted back in and I heard him give the order to go round the back. I was done for.

He looked out at me again. 'Give up, Moham, you're nicked. You've got some explaining to do, lad. Wait till Rafiq finds out. He'll nail your balls to the wall.'

Bastard. All I'd done was hang about with a few mates. I hadn't even had so much as a fag. Alright, there were a few girls involved – white girls. I hadn't done anything with them, only talk. But that was a crime in my culture, and I would definitely pay for it.

As I got to the bottom of the pipe, the back gate swung open and through it strode two men. One I didn't recognize. The other I did, much to my relief. It was Qaisar. A quiet and deeply religious man, he'd married my cousin Ayesha a couple of years previously in a ceremony in Tajak and they'd come to live in Hawesmill, just down the road from where the doss-house was. Qaisar had taken a shine to me, perhaps recognizing that I wasn't exactly flavour of the month among the relatives. He was always kind and generous. He'd a good sense of humour too, which he only showed to a few people. He was a passionate cricket fan and would bowl ball after ball at me in the backstreet behind Hamilton Terrace, using upturned plastic milk crates for stumps. I wasn't much of a batsman, but Qaisar was patient and showed me a few tricks he'd learned on the sun-baked wickets of north-west Pakistan. He'd even promised to take me to a Test match at Old Trafford or Headingley. It hadn't happened so far, but I lived in hope.

Now he marched right up to me and grabbed me by the shoulder.

'What've you been up to?! Moham, I thought better of you than this.'

He gestured inside at the three sobbing girls and their two Asian friends, now looking far less confident and cocky than they had done just a few hours earlier.

'I can't believe you've been mixing with white women,' he said, looking the angriest I'd ever seen him. 'You know it's *haraam*. White girls are just trouble. Big trouble. Look at them. They're dressed like prostitutes. You know what a prostitute is, Moham? No? Well, I hope you never find out.'

I bit my lip and tried not to cry. Qaisar was like a big brother to me and I couldn't bear him shouting like this.

Yasir came into the yard and came right up to my face, fixing me dead in the eye.

'You're gonna get a thrashing, little brother,' he sneered. 'When you-know-who finds out, you won't stand up straight for a week.'

'That's enough, Yasir!' Qaisar said, shoving him away from me. 'I'll deal with this. Go home and keep your mouth shut.'

Yasir may have been Ayesha's brother, but in the family pecking order he was below her husband. He slunk off, giving me one last dirty look before he left. Qaisar told Haani and Sadeeq and the white girls to clear off too. They didn't need a second reminder, shooting out of the back gate like rats from a trap.

'You've missed mosque as well, haven't you?'

Meekly, I nodded my head.

'That's bad, Moham. Really, really bad. I'm amazed Rafiq hasn't noticed, you idiot. What were you thinking about?'

'I dunno,' I mumbled. 'Haani and Sadeeq said it was cool, and these girls were nice, honest, and we were having a laugh, and ...'

'Shut up, Moham!' Qaisar looked really mad again. 'I don't want to hear it. You've been hanging around with sluts and not going to mosque. Allah, His name be praised, has got His eye on you, son. You do anything like this again and you will burn, I promise you.'

I looked at my trainers, scuffed from where I'd shinned down the drainpipe.

'You won't tell Rafiq, will you? Please, Qaisar. You know what he'll do.'

'Not this time, but if I ever catch you again, Moham …'

'I'm dead sorry. I won't do it again.'

'You'd better not. Anyway … when are we watching the Test match?'

I brightened instantly. 'Soon as you like! Pakistan are gonna thrash England, aren't they, Qaisar?'

'You'd better believe it, kid. I'll have a look at the fixtures, see when we can next get across. We'll have a top day out, eh?'

I wanted to cry again, but out of happiness this time. Qaisar was cool, and I would keep my promise to him. I knew he wouldn't tell Rafiq, and even when he cuffed the side of my head as I walked out of the yard, I knew I would be OK as long as he was around to protect me.

In the event Rafiq did find out, though, a day or two after the drama. Hawesmill isn't a place you can keep secrets, and someone – probably Haani, Sadeeq or Yasir – let the cat out of the bag. Rafiq dragged me out of the house and onto the street, and in the fight that followed I managed to lose both my shirt and trousers. I ran down the road and hid behind a parked car as Rafiq screamed and shouted.

When he'd calmed down, Jasmine sneaked out of the back gate and brought me a shirt and jeans. She'd seen the whole thing from an upstairs window and couldn't bear to watch her brother in trouble again.

I walked around for hours that night, but when I arrived home Rafiq was waiting and once again I was imprisoned in the outside bog after an incredible bollocking featuring both Rafiq and Abida. She was embarrassed that her late husband's son could behave in such an un-Islamic way. I wanted to tell them that it wasn't because I wanted sex, or anything like it, with these girls. I just needed to know how it felt to be white. But I didn't tell them. That kind of remark would've seen my nose bent like a banana all over again.

I kept my word and never went near Haani and Sadeeq, or any white girls, again. I literally put my head down – not daring to look up if I felt there was a woman close by me on the street. Life became a strict routine of mosque-home-mosque-home-mosque-home-mosque-home-mosque-bed, using the backstreets wherever possible to avoid Rafiq.

Luckily, Qaisar and Ayesha were kind, allowing me to visit whenever I liked. Although Qaisar was religious and could be very serious at times, Ayesha was still her old fun-loving self and I always enjoyed seeing her. I'd usually come in through the back gate and when she was in the kitchen she'd have the Ritz biscuits out before I'd reached the door. She knew I loved them and would buy them specially for me.

At that time Ayesha had a small child and another one on the way – no doubt there were plans for a big family, if Qaisar had anything to do with it. She seemed happy with her lot and she was still a very sociable girl. She was well known around Hawesmill for her stories and her loud laugh. Sometimes I saw Qaisar looking at her when she was laughing with me over something stupid and I wondered what he made of his lively, noisy wife. But he had a sense of humour, as I've said, and he could wisecrack with the best of them. To me, they were a perfect couple and I loved spending as much time with them as I could.

In the meantime I prayed fervently to Allah to forgive my sins and listened carefully to the verses from the Qur'an that I still didn't understand. Difficult though it was, I tried not to think about Debbie's cleavage or Carol's shapely legs. I did everything that a good little Muslim boy should do to please his elders, and any other Muslim family would've been proud of me. But not mine. Rafiq's quest for perfection and his unstoppable bullying meant he was never satisfied with my efforts.

I'd also started to annoy Rafiq by being bold enough to ask Abida several questions about my mum, but she would always change the subject. She didn't want to hear anything about another woman. But hanging about white people had stoked the fire of my imagination. More than ever, I was deeply curious about what they were like and what they did, and how I might have fitted into that world if things had been different. Increasingly I felt myself alienated from the community I'd grown up in, and this manifested itself in embarrassing questions to Abida. I'm guessing my mum was the last topic of conversation she wanted. I was young, though, and felt no shame in asking.

Abida obviously told Rafiq, and one night he summoned me into the front room where he often sat, feet up, reading the paper while Abida cooked, washed, cleaned and dealt with the children.

'What're you doing?' he snarled in his usual gruff tone. 'I want a word with you ...'

'I'm going to mosque all the time and praying very hard for forgiveness,' I said, not wanting to catch his eye.

'Are you now? Well, I'm not sure it's enough for the sins you've committed. You need a deeper understanding of God if you are to make peace with Him, yes?'

'Yes, Uncle Rafiq.'

'So this is what I've decided for you: you will go away for a week. There is a trip going from the mosque to Blackburn. There, you will eat, sleep and pray in the mosque, every day, and at night you will go out onto the streets, looking for sinners to pray for. Understood?'

'Yes, Uncle Rafiq. Can I ask you a question?'

'If it's about your mother, then no. I don't want to hear any more talk of white women in this house.'

'No, it wasn't that ... I just wanted to know when I was going to Blackburn.'

In response he threw a black bin liner at me. 'You're going tonight. Get upstairs and pack enough stuff in there for a week. Then I'll walk you down to the minibus – I want to make sure you don't run off with any white women.'

He laughed at his own little joke and I managed a sickly smile.

A week on my knees praying didn't sound the most appealing of holidays, but actually I was delighted. A week anywhere, even a mosque in the arse-end of Blackburn, was a week away from Hawesmill and Rafiq. Frankly, I couldn't wait.

Once I'd thrown a few clothes into the bag I was ready, and Rafiq marched me down to the mosque, where a group of the more religious elements around Hawesmill were waiting.

'Here he is – the penitent sinner.' Rafiq gave me a small shove in the back, casting me into a circle of disapproving looks. I'd half-hoped that Haani and Sadeeq would be among the party, but there was no sign of them. Perhaps their families had arranged another kind of punishment for them – or maybe other parents weren't as bullying and vengeful as Rafiq.

Trips like this, going from mosque to mosque across the north-west and sometimes into Yorkshire, were regular occurrences then and still are today. Seven or eight men travel to hear preachers and say prayers in the mosque and fit in a bit of missionary work on the streets. You have to be a certain age to go unaccompanied and I was the youngest of this lot by about 15 years. No one spoke to me as I slung my belongings into the back of the minibus and climbed in. I didn't care. It was nice to be going somewhere different.

Hawesmill isn't a million miles from Blackburn and within 45 minutes we'd arrived at the familiar two-shabby-houses-knocked-through-style mosque on the fringes of Whalley Range. There wasn't any time for introductions other than the usual '*Salaam*'; we were straight into a two-hour session of prayers followed by a talk from a visiting preacher granting us higher powers on our mission to seek out sinners and get them to repent.

I have to confess to being Islam's most unsuccessful missionary. I had nothing to say to anyone. However, the men in the party thought nothing of approaching hard-looking lads hanging around outside corner shops.

'*Salaam alaykum*,' they'd say, 'Peace be upon you,' as the teenagers pulled hard on their cigarettes and narrowed their eyes like cartoon cowboys.

'Have you boys been to mosque today?' they'd ask. 'No? Don't you think you should, for it says in the Holy Book that those who reject Faith shall be companions of the Fire. You understand what that means?'

'Get stuffed, knobhead,' was a typical response, but the missionaries would press on regardless.

'Those who believe fight in the cause of Allah, and those who reject faith fight in the cause of Evil,' the men would proclaim. Giving the youths a blessing, they would move on.

I loitered at the back, hoping I wouldn't be noticed and made fun of. While the missionaries were lecturing another unclean soul about the benefits of Paradise, I did my best to look holy. I also made sure I didn't nod off while listening to the various preachers in the mosque. Besides, some of what was being said was actually going in, and I found myself regularly praying to God for forgiveness. Rafiq would've been pleased to know that his little brainwashing plan was beginning to have an effect; by the end of the week I felt closer to the religion I'd been born into than I'd ever done before and I vowed to stay as pure as a 12-year-old boy with yo-yoing hormones possibly could.

I returned to Hawesmill feeling spiritually uplifted. Every time I passed a woman on the street I whispered, 'God forgive me,' and looked away.

There was no chance of going back to see the white girls; Haani and Sadeeq weren't around anymore and I daren't risk an excursion to the empty doss-house alone. Even if Rafiq didn't see me, God would, and I didn't want to fall out of favour with Him.

Besides, I was being kept out of trouble with work; while I was away Abida had asked Fatima if there was anything I could do for Dilawar in the shop and he'd taken me on as a lowly shelf-filler and produce-sorter. For this I was paid next to nothing, but at least I was occupied and under surveillance, which must have kept Rafiq happy.

One afternoon when I returned home to get changed out of my work clothes before prayers, Abida asked me to come into the kitchen. She beckoned me to sit at the small corner table and brought over a cup of tea.

'Mohammed,' she said, in a kindly tone, 'do you remember when you went to Pakistan as a little boy?'

I had to think hard. I had only been a small child then and the memories were vague and fleeting. I told her about trying to shoot the moon and she laughed.

'I know you really enjoyed it there,' she said. 'You felt really at home. I was thinking … have you ever thought of going back?'

I hadn't. A week in Blackburn was as exotic as it ever got. Since Dad had died, first-hand news from Pakistan had been less frequent and the country hadn't seemed to come up as often in conversation. Occasionally, we'd crowd into Fatima's back room to watch videos sent from Tajak. Seeing scenes of weddings, harvest time and other celebrations brought back memories of my three years in Pakistan, but I hadn't thought I'd ever get the chance to go back.

'How do you mean?' I said.

'Well, if the chance came to go for a holiday there, would you fancy it?'

My stomach turned over with excitement. Pakistan! It was so lovely and warm there, and what I remembered of it gave me a comfortable glow.

'I'd love to go, *Ami*,' I said, 'but I haven't got any money. How would I get there?'

'Oh, Mohammed, don't be silly!' she said brightly. 'Cousin Yasir is going on business to Islamabad and he'll take you along for a few weeks. We've found the money to pay for your fare, so don't worry about that.'

Abida was rarely horrible to me and today she was being extra nice. I wondered if she was in some way trying to make amends for Rafiq's ongoing nastiness. But I also knew that she did everything her brother told her. I wouldn't be going to Pakistan without him knowing, and if he had anything to do with it, it wouldn't be a holiday – far from it. But Abida seemed sincere enough, so I accepted the offer with thanks. Yasir could be a bit of an idiot at times – over the white girls, for example – but usually he was OK and I didn't mind his company if he was in a good mood.

The following day Abida told me the tickets were booked and I'd be flying in under 10 days' time. I could hardly wait.

Jasmine wasn't quite so delighted. 'It's not fair,' she moaned. 'How come you cause loads of trouble and get rewarded for it?'

'Shuddup, you … I don't cause trouble. It wasn't my fault about them white girls.'

'Yeah, well, I never do *anything* wrong, and I have to stay in here cleaning up. So why can't *I* go instead of you? Or come with you?'

'I dunno,' I replied, but I did know. For years now Jasmine had played the role of a 'little mother', cooking, washing, cleaning, running round after the younger ones. School wasn't even mentioned for her either, but at least I could get a bit of fresh air on the walk to the mosque. She was in all day, every day, and for a girl approaching her teens that must've been a killer. At the time, though, I didn't consider that she should have a different sort of life from the one she was living.

Rafiq seemed pleased that I'd decided to go. I got the impression that if I'd refused, my mind would've been changed, swiftly and violently. But in the days leading up to my departure he was all smiles, telling me what a great trip I'd have and how everyone in Tajak was looking forward to meeting me again now I'd grown up. Of course, he also warned me that any bad behaviour would bring shame upon the family both in Hawesmill and Tajak.

'Remember,' he growled, 'there are people watching. News travels fast. If I hear you're causing trouble …' His words tailed off, but left me in no doubt what he meant.

The days leading up to the departure dragged on, and the closer I got to it, the more I realized how boring my life really was. Mosque, shop and home, those were my only destinations, and after the white girls incident I was forced to spend most of my time alone. Rafiq made sure that no friends would be calling at Hamilton Terrace either now or in the future.

My loneliness was made worse by the sense of confinement in these narrow-minded streets. Beyond Hawesmill there are huge stretches of wild moorland, but I'd never walked over them, nor had anyone else from my street. Going for an afternoon hike on the hills is unthinkable in my community; it smacks too much of enjoyment. No wonder I couldn't wait to be among the spacious villages and fertile open plains of northwest Pakistan. People lived much closer to the land over there and I wanted to breathe freely once more, even if only for a short time.

Finally, the day came. Abida handed me a battered suitcase that had belonged to Dad and told me to pack for two weeks. I threw in every set of *salwar kameez* I had, plus my *topi* hat. I didn't want to look like an outsider. I'd heard all the tales of visitors to Pakistan being laughed at by the locals for their Western ways. Abida gave me another suitcase filled with bits and pieces of old clothing, mainly Dad's, for the relatives to share out. It felt strange taking these last physical reminders away from Hawesmill, but perhaps it was the right thing to do.

Yasir knocked on the door at about 7 a.m. and after a quick goodbye to Abida and Jasmine, I climbed into the back of a brown Austin Maxi driven by Dilawar and we set off for Heathrow. Rafiq didn't bother to leave his bed to say farewell. I wasn't upset about that.

As we joined the junction for the M6 I leaned back in my seat and thanked God for forgiving me and supplying this holiday of a lifetime as a reward for my good behaviour. Yasir was in a good mood, too, and we chatted in English all the way to the outskirts of London.

By the time we had walked through passport control and down the walkway into the Pakistan International Airlines Boeing 747 to Islamabad, I was absolutely buzzing. The plane was full of families making journeys to see relatives back home and you could almost taste the excitement. I nipped in front of Yasir and claimed the window seat; I knew he wouldn't mind that a thrilled 12-year-old had grabbed the bird's eye view. I had been on a plane before, of course, but I remembered nothing of it and so this was like my first time.

When the 747 taxied down the runway and hauled itself into the air, I experienced a surge of adrenaline that I'd never felt before. It literally took my breath away. I found myself staring, open-mouthed, at the ground disappearing below.

Yasir smiled, and touched my arm. 'This is gonna be a great trip, little brother,' he said, 'one that you'll never forget as long as you live.'

How right he was, especially about the second part.

Chapter Seven

All that flight I kept checking to see if I was really this lucky – lucky to be going on a proper holiday in a hot country and even luckier to have escaped the grim confines of Hawesmill and the merciless Rafiq. I never stopped nattering to Yasir and must've driven him mad with my incessant questions about Pakistan and Tajak. He answered them all with good humour and patience, only faltering when I wondered how long we would be staying. I'd asked Abida this, but she'd been vague.

'Ummm, three weeks maybe,' Yasir said. 'Could be longer. I've got serious business there, Moham, and it might not be very easy to sort out. But you'll be OK, there will be plenty to do. You gotta remember this, little brother – you belong to Tajak. You're part of it.'

He stared at me through his thick-framed glasses and smiled. I knew what he was trying to say – that I was a Pakistani boy through and through, despite everything. In his own way he was being kind. But telling me that I 'belonged' to somewhere in Pakistan only deepened my feeling of not belonging anywhere, and the old questions about my mum flashed through my mind once more. Where was she? Why hadn't she come to find us? What would life be like if she had? The harder I tried to suppress them, the more fiercely they nagged at me.

However, I was determined that nothing would spoil this holiday, not even the gnawing concerns over my mum. So when the plane touched down at Islamabad International Airport and the doors finally opened after what seemed like an eternally long, noisy and impatient wait, I allowed the furnace-blast of dry heat that hit me full in the face to burn away all the memories of Hawesmill. The rain, the mean little terrace streets, Rafiq, the subway, shop and mosque, they all melted into a pool of nothing.

The excitement inside the plane as the doors opened was overwhelming. British Asian families had saved up for months and years for this moment. Finally they were home, and the celebrations that would follow on the other side of the customs barrier inside the airport would be rapturous.

Having been to Pakistan before and seen the videos from Tajak, I knew that I was in for a culture shock. As we waited at the baggage carousel I noticed how dark the handlers were compared to the people back home. 'Another 50 years in Hawesmill and we'll be as white as anyone else,' I thought.

Then I reeled back in shock. Creeping towards the carousel was a collection of beggars, most of them in rags, many of them deformed. Some held out babies and children with arms and legs missing. I don't know how they'd managed to get into this part of the airport, but here they were, crying and pleading for money at our feet as we waited for our bulging suitcases. I'd thought Hawesmill was poor, but I'd never seen anything like this before and, to my shame, I just stared at them in horror.

Yasir put his hand in his pocket and gave a one-eyed, one-legged beggar some loose change. I wondered what the man would do with a claw full of British copper and silver. At least it had the effect of getting rid of him, and we hurried through passport control with our bags, shaken by what we'd just witnessed.

Beyond the barrier which separated passengers from the rest of Pakistan stood hundreds of expectant relatives all scanning the newly arrived for familiar faces. I knew that white people laughed at us because we 'all looked the same' to them. For a moment, I knew what they meant: these men were uniformly dark-skinned and had moustaches, and the older ones were deeply lined from years in the sun. Unsurprisingly, there were no women present; it wasn't their place to go to an airport unless they were travelling themselves.

I didn't see a soul I recognized until Yasir, striding ahead, suddenly raised his arms to a group of men and ran towards them.

'Ajmal! Hussein! *Salaam alaykum*! Oh, it's so good to see you! Here we are at last!'

Yasir fell into their embraces and a round of heavy back-slapping and hand-pumping took place. I didn't recognize them, but in front of me were Ajmal and Hussein Khan, my dad's younger brothers. Alongside them stood a couple of shy-eyed kids who'd come along for the ride – grandchildren, I guessed, for these men looked old to me. As it turned out, the kids were actually their children; the Pakistani sun does a good job of ageing skin in double-quick time.

'And this, uncles, is Mohammed, son of Ahmed, God rest his soul.'

Yasir pushed me into the arms of the men I'd last seen as a small child. They embraced me like a long-lost son. Hussein wept and said prayers for the soul of my dad. It felt like the day of the funeral all over again, but at least Hussein was holding me with what felt like genuine emotion and not just out of self-pity

'Welcome to Pakistan, Mohammed,' he said, eyes brimming with tears. 'I hope you will be happy here.'

He spoke quickly, in heavy Pashto that I could barely understand. With his long white beard, he reminded me of pictures I'd seen of Father Christmas.

Ajmal nodded vigorously. He was shorter than Hussein and clean-shaven. He too seemed nice and genuinely pleased to see me, though I was learning not to judge a book by its cover.

The kids said nothing, just stared at the two foreigners who'd stepped off the giant silver bird from England.

'Moham's been having a hard time in England, haven't you?' Yasir looked at me and I nodded dumbly. 'He's been making some bad choices, uncles. As a family, we've all agreed to help him find the right path.'

'*Inshallah*, if Allah wills it, Mohammed,' said Ajmal gravely. 'We will help you to find this once again. Have no fear.'

I smiled, wondering what they meant, but my Pashto wasn't strong enough to reply. I smiled and nodded again, hoping that they wouldn't try too hard with the righteousness and would let me get on and enjoy my holiday in peace.

Hussein and Ajmal led us to the airport car park, keeping up an unceasing flow of banter with Yasir. From what I could understand, they were asking about relatives in England and whether life was still good 'over there'. To say otherwise would be to lose face and admit defeat. I imagine Yasir told them that Hawesmill was thriving these days, that its residents were prosperous and happy, and that the sun always shone on this lucky little corner of Lancashire. I often wonder why members of close families lie to one another in this way. Maybe it's a method of protection – protecting yourself and your loved ones from unpleasant truths. Or perhaps it's about making your bed and lying in it, because no one wants to admit they've got it wrong.

We piled into an ancient Ford van, converted for passenger use. It must've been at least 30 years old, but was in good condition, body-wise. The dry climate protects old vehicles against rust, and Pakistan is full of them. That said, the van chugged and spluttered its way out of Islamabad airport like a 60-a-dayer and I wondered when – or even if – we would make it to Tajak.

The snail's pace gave us visitors the chance to really soak in the scenery. I don't think I've ever filled my eyes so fully with such chaotic beauty. We spent most of the time on a main road, and the view was superb. Brightly coloured trucks, several storeys high and laden with produce of all kinds, passed us every minute. Drivers were smoking cigarettes, arms hanging carelessly out of windows, while other passengers clung to the outsides or sat right on top of the produce. If they fell it was certain death, but they seemed as relaxed and happy as their driver. Horns of all descriptions honked every millisecond and drivers cut each other up without a care. Traffic signals rarely functioned, so an overworked and impatient cop would attempt to direct traffic at bustling junctions.

All this human drama was going on under the bluest skies I'd ever seen. In contrast, the sun rarely shone over Hawesmill, or at least that's how it felt. There were always clouds, great dark galleons of rain scudding over the town from the Pennines or the Irish Sea, casting deep shadows and promising trouble. Here, it seemed, there were no such shadows. The plane trees lining the roads reached up joyously to the sky and the warmth soaked into you like a hot bath at the end of a hard day. I was tired from the long flight, but still buzzing; I wanted Pakistan to fold me up and protect me, and for the first time in years I felt safe from harm.

When I tried speaking to Hussein and Ajmal in Pashto, the kids giggled, and a memory floated back of a journey from an airport to the north of England many years before. I switched to English with Yasir, which caused the little ones to stare open-mouthed at the Pakistanis who spoke like aliens. Not that we were very Pakistani these days; we stopped at a roadside café for tea and the owner of the shack immediately clocked us for visitors, noticing our clothes and the shade of our skin. In England all this information would've been processed by a quick glance, but here on the outskirts of Islamabad no one thought twice about giving you a long leisurely stare.

'It's OK, little brother,' said Yasir, noticing my discomfort, 'they're just curious, that's all. You're gonna get a lot of this over the next few weeks. Get used to it.'

I wasn't sure if I could. It was a penetrating gaze that seemed to reach into your soul. I'd seen Rafiq give it me a couple of times and assumed it was just him being weird. Maybe not … I didn't feel at all comfortable with the thought of people staring at me for two weeks. I vowed to keep my gaze averted whenever I saw strangers, just like I'd done on the streets of Hawesmill after the white girls incident.

'Oh, here we go,' said Yasir, as the Ford started to slow down, 'we must be close now. Look, Moham – up ahead. You'll never see anything like this in England.'

I leaned forward and saw two large towers on either side of the road. In between was a red-and-white striped barrier and in front of that a gang of men in military uniforms, holding up their hands in the universal signal for 'halt'.

'What is it?' I whispered anxiously.

'Roadblock,' Yasir said. 'Don't worry, it's fine.'

The Ford pulled up alongside one of the soldiers and Hussein spoke quickly to him as he pushed a sheaf of papers through the window. He gestured to us in the back and the soldier said something I didn't catch.

'He wants your passports,' Hussein said. 'All routine.'

Yasir handed over the precious booklets for inspection. I looked out of the window, trying not to stare too hard at the machine guns the soldiers gripped firmly as they wandered around the bus, occasionally bending down to examine the underside. Beyond the roadblock was a perimeter fence made of four thick rolls of coiled barbed wire. In the distance I could see several camouflage-painted fighter jets sitting on a runway.

Satisfied, the soldiers lifted the barrier and waved us on.

After a few hundred yards, I plucked up the courage to ask Yasir what it was all about.

'Kamra air force base,' he replied. 'Security's really tight. There are guys up in Afghanistan who'd love to get their hands on some of the weaponry in there. The military double-checks everyone, even those they see every day. Isn't that right, Hussein?'

Hussein nodded, his Father Christmas beard bobbing up and down. 'I don't mind the military being around,' he said. 'Keeps the bandits away.'

Yasir explained that Hussein was a truck driver and that hijackings of vehicles were not uncommon in Pakistan. People were generally poor, he said, and if they could supplement their income by selling on things that had literally fallen off the back of a lorry, they would. But not so much in this area. The military saw to that. In fact, tension was very high here. Just over the border in Afghanistan were the famed and feared *mujahideen*. For a long time now this group of rebels had been fighting the invading Soviet army. I knew very little about them, despite talk around Hawesmill of the brave Muslim freedom fighters who'd fought the Soviets to a standstill in Afghanistan. As far as I was concerned, it could've been happening on Jupiter.

Confronted with the reality in this remote corner of north-west Pakistan, it was my turn to stare like a local.

Two or three miles past Kamra the Ford turned off the main road and down a bumpy, dusty dirt track.

Yasir nudged me. 'We're here, little brother! This is it – Tajak. Don't you remember?'

I remembered nothing. Nothing about the strange mixture of newly-built houses and shacks, nothing about the men driving donkey carts or sitting idly outside grocer's shops, watching the world go by. There was nothing about the large walls of the compounds which housed three or four related families that reminded me of my time here, and even when my nostrils contracted at the terrible smell of shit that came from the open sewers running alongside the road, I recalled nothing of that sickly-sweet odour. It was all brand new to me.

Tajak looked rundown and dirty, yet there were some very fine houses dotted here and there. I wondered how people could afford to build them when all around seemed to be poverty and decay.

A lad of about my age stacking up watermelons outside a shop paused as we passed. I caught his eye and smiled. 'If I'd stayed,' I thought, 'that would have been me, piling up fruit for a few rupees.'

We passed through the centre of Tajak and continued for about half a mile before slowing down.

Yasir started laughing. 'Look at this,' he shouted in English, 'the welcoming party! Blimey, Moham, they think we were the Royal Family. Look at them!'

Up ahead was a line of about 20 adults, mainly women, and the same number of children. The grown-ups were waving, the children jumping up and down and dancing on the spot.

'Home again,' said Ajmal, smiling.

These people must've been waiting for us for an hour or more in the baking heat. I couldn't believe they'd turned out to greet us. As the Ford stopped they crowded in at the window, knocking on the glass. It was so different from the reception we'd got in Hawesmill, when our bags had simply been dumped on the pavement on a cold winter's night.

We got out and the crowd rushed forward. I was pulled into a series of embraces and the sides of my cheeks were squeezed hard by women who couldn't believe I was the same little boy who'd toddled around the village so many years before.

'He's so grown up!'

'He's the image of his father, God have mercy on him!'

'Oh, he's so pale – look at him. He needs a good dose of the sun!'

A tall, slim long-haired woman stepped forward and took me by the hand. 'What he needs is a long cool drink, isn't it, Mohammed? Come inside, you must be tired.'

She led me through the compound gate and round the side of a brick wall which shielded the inner courtyard from prying eyes. Inside there were four houses built in a square, but seemingly all connected by passageways. She took me into one – small, but very neat and well designed – and passed me a glass of clear liquid that tasted like lemonade but not quite. I was too shy to ask what it was and instead drank deeply from the glass, draining every drop.

'Now that's better, isn't it?' the woman said. 'Bet you've never had watermelon sherbet before. It's my own recipe. You look like a human being again. Oh, by the way I'm Alia. I'm married to your Uncle Ajmal.'

'So you're my aunty?'

'That's right,' she said sweetly. 'Don't you remember me? No, of course you don't. You were only little. I looked after you a lot back then. You were a lovely boy. Bet you still are.'

I blushed and she laughed. 'Red cheeks! I've never seen a Pakistani boy blush red before. That's so funny. I'm so glad you've come, Mohammed. We all are. We've been dying to meet you again. You can stay in my house while you're here. Come and go as you please. We just want you to enjoy yourself, that's all, and be a good boy.'

'I promise,' I said, and I meant it. There was something about Alia I thought I could trust. How she'd taken my hand and led me out of the mêlée, the way she'd smiled at me and brushed back her long dark hair, they were all echoes of my long-lost mum.

Instantly I felt tears well up. This was, and still is, a common reaction when someone is kind to me. I still find generosity hard to accept and I'm usually wary of it. On the rare occasions it is heartfelt, I'm deeply touched and have trouble fighting back the tears. I was struggling then, even as Alia teased me about my blushes and offered to make me another sherbet. She was a wise woman when it came to children; she had two of her own. So when she saw my distress, she cuddled me to her.

'Hey, Mohammed, don't cry. I want you to be happy here, not sad. What's the matter?'

I couldn't tell her, not then. Maybe later on, when I knew her better, I'd say something about the way I felt and what was happening to me in England. Then I realized – she probably already knew. 'Be a good boy …' I didn't doubt that behind my back I was a hot topic of conversation around Hawesmill, but until now I wasn't aware that news of the boy with the white mother and the devil in his heart had reached this remote village. Alia looked as though she didn't believe a word of it, but how could I be sure? I never knew who I could trust, and while Alia looked the sort of person you could share your deepest secrets with, how would I know if she was passing on information to Rafiq, or Abida or Fatima?

Now she was stroking the side of my face and taking my hand. 'Come on, let's introduce you round,' she said, 'though I don't expect you to remember everyone's name. It's a big family.'

She led me back to the front of the compound where the relatives were still hovering around Yasir, fussing with his luggage and hanging onto his every word. She clapped her hands and asked everyone to be quiet for a moment. It was just after midday and the heat was intense. Sweat was pouring down my forehead and onto my face, stinging my eyes. I was beginning to feel the effects of jet-lag and just wanted to lie down somewhere cool, but greeting everyone properly was the height of good manners. I was keen to make the right impression. I salaamed and shook hands with a series of grubby cheeky-looking kids whose names I instantly forgot, but would come to learn as time passed.

Then it was the adults. I greeted Grandma and Granddad with the respect their age deserved. Grandma seemed especially pleased to see me, and I guessed she'd had a lot to do with me during my first visit here as a small boy.

Then it was the turn of 'Little Fatima', the twin sister of the Hawesmill Fatima. I never did find out her real name; her mother had jokingly called her 'Little Fatima' because she was the younger by a minute or so, which seemed a bit unfair, and the name had stuck.

Her daughter, Farida, was next to greet me, a lively-looking girl with ponytails on either side of her head. She must've been in her mid-twenties, but there appeared to be no children clinging to her *jilbab*.

'Hi, Mohammed,' she said, her brown eyes all big and welcoming, 'it's great to have you here. I'm really looking forward to hearing about England. I've heard it's amazing. Is it as good as everyone says?'

'Well …' I began, but then caught Yasir's reproving look and hesitated.

Farida pushed down her bottom lip in a pretend sulk. 'Awww, don't spoil it,' she said. 'You've got to say it's fantastic. Come on – say it.'

The relatives were crowding round to hear the verdict on England from the horse's mouth. How could I disappoint them? They didn't want to know about the rain and the racism, the boredom and the bullying and the poverty and unemployment. England's streets were paved with gold, according to those in the know in Tajak. Even an irritating adolescent like me knew not to spoil it for them.

'It's great,' I said limply. 'Fantastic. Just how you imagine it to be.'

The family broke out into collective smiles and I was patted on the back for telling it like it wasn't. Alia put her arm around my shoulders and gently squeezed me to her. I felt certain she knew the truth about my situation in Hawesmill.

'And this,' she said, 'is your Uncle Imran.'

I turned to face a tall, thin stringy man with a face creased by the sun into a permanently fierce expression. His hooded eyes were hard and unforgiving, and he stood slightly to one side of everyone else, as if he'd been forced to attend this silly little party and would rather be doing anything other than meeting two foreigners who claimed to be Pakistani. Immediately, he made me feel nervous.

'I … I didn't know I had another uncle,' I stammered. 'I thought it was just Hussein and Ajmal.'

'It is,' Imran said. 'I'm not your uncle at all. You will know me as Rafiq's brother.'

Of course. The same whip-like build and sullen, hawkish expression. No wonder he made me edgy. It felt as though a cloud had just appeared across the sun, turning the afternoon ominously chilly.

Yasir engaged Imran in conversation, clapping him on the back now and again to reinforce a point. I felt they were talking about me and I turned away, determined not to get caught in the hate-filled stream of Imran's gaze, and spoke to a couple of my little cousins who were playing in and out of the Ford van.

The welcoming party carried on long into that evening. A goat had been killed in our honour and was slowly roasting in a large outdoor cooking pot that contained a delicious-smelling curry sauce. Everyone was milling round – neighbours, friends and relatives alike – and the welcome was as warm as the evening meal. Imran had taken himself off. I didn't bother to ask where he'd gone. If I thought about him too hard, a little wave of anxiety would creep into my stomach, and I didn't want anything to spoil my holiday. I decided to ignore him when he was around.

After the gathering had broken up I was directed to a bedroom in Ajmal and Alia's house. I was fascinated by the way they lived. The houses themselves weren't large, and furniture was minimal, but they were all connected by a series of openings curtained by a hessian-style material. This meant relatives could come and go into each other's houses at will, so their way of life was very communal. Each house had its own small vegetable patch, and orange trees were dotted in clumps under the walls of the compound. There was a small enclosure for a handful of goats, which provided meat and milk, and chickens ran freely around the houses.

Yasir and I were billeted in the same room. He fell asleep immediately, worn out by the long journey and full of hearty food. I lay on the bed, listening to the noises of a warm Pakistani night. Somewhere in the distance a dog howled eerily and moths fluttered and bumped against the oil lamp by the window. I smelled the heavy perfume of the jasmine and lotus flowers that draped themselves down the walls of the compound. Slowly I sank into sleep, excited and eager to start the holiday in the heart of the country and culture that had claimed me as its own.

Chapter Eight

The next few days were spent exploring my immediate surroundings. I was struck by how much space there was and how light and airy everything seemed. There was no glass in any of the windows, and a cool breeze blew in through the thin mesh coverings. This was pleasant, especially when you were lying in a bedroom during the heat of mid-afternoon.

Most of all, I loved the garden. It was huge, much bigger than any garden I'd ever seen before, and varied in its uses. A cow tied to a tree was milked daily while chickens ran around its hooves. Alia and Little Fatima cooked outside using the traditional *tandoor*, the big circular clay oven used all over Pakistan. There was a smaller version inside for use during the rainy season. The women spent many hours outside and I'd often seen them sewing clothes or putting oil into their hair in the shade of a grapevine which had spread itself thickly over a wooden frame. This was my favourite part of the garden.

Soon I began sleeping outside. I'd carry my light and portable rope-slatted bed outside, then stare up at the skies in search of shooting stars until my eyelids drooped and I fell asleep. Little Fatima told me that a shooting star was God throwing a stone at the devil, and I completely believed her. One night there was an unexpected and heavy rain shower, but that didn't mess up my outdoor sleeping arrangements. I simply hauled a big sheet of thick plastic over myself and lay on my bed, listening to the raindrops thudding down. The little kids thought I was mad, but being outside at night was so much more pleasant than a damp, stuffy bedroom in Hawesmill and I wanted to make the most of it while I could.

The toilet facilities were also located in the garden, but only for women. Men would squat in the fields and I was taught to copy them by Ajmal, who went mad when he saw me peeing against the compound wall.

'Mohammed! What the hell are you doing?!' he yelled, running towards me full pelt. I thought he was going to bollock me for weeing up against the wall, but it wasn't that at all.

'No! No! No!' he shouted. 'Not like that! Only dirty dogs piss against walls. You don't stand up – you must squat.'

I shook my head in disbelief, so he demonstrated, pulling down his baggy *salwar kameez* trousers and squatting with his long shawl over his head so that his entire body was covered. Eventually a golden trickle of pee emerged from the bottom of the shawl and trickled into the dust. I laughed, but Ajmal was perfectly serious and went straight back in to get me a shawl of my own. From that moment on that's how I went to the loo, and squatting shapes in the fields around Tajak became an everyday sight. If you ever walk in a field in Pakistan, be very careful where you put your feet …

One of the first things I was obliged to do was visit Dad's grave. Abida had said several times how important this was. Although I wasn't looking forward to it, I wanted to do it as soon as possible. I knew word would reach England eventually of my time in Pakistan and I wanted to prove to Abida and Rafiq that I was a good Muslim, capable of doing my duty by my dead father.

On the day of the visit Yasir came with me and we walked to the graveyard, which was right by the main mosque in Tajak. I poked around for a bit, looking at the gravestones and wondering what the Arabic writing said. Yasir and I had no idea where Dad was buried, so we asked a local man who was weeding the graveyard and he led us to the grave.

I'd rehearsed some prayers to say, but when I reached the unkempt plot of earth, words just failed me. I stood there for what seemed like ages, holding my hands palm upwards in the Islamic way, but no prayers would come. It had been two years since Dad's death, but the pain was still raw and real. Tears pricked my eyes as I stared at the gravestone, but there was anger mixed with the sadness.

Standing beside me, Yasir smiled. He could see I was in distress and that I was muttering and holding my hands up in prayer. I expect he was pleased to see me fulfilling my duty to my late father so piously. Little did he know that I was almost cursing Dad for dying and abandoning us to uncaring relatives.

'Why the hell did you die, Dad?' I whispered. 'Why did you leave me and Jasmine in such a mess? Why did you make Mum go away? Why did Rafiq come along and ruin everything? Why, why, why?'

Standing there in the blazing heat of a Pakistani afternoon, in that dusty, overgrown and unkempt graveyard crawling with lizards and spiders and God knows what else, I'd never felt so alone. Even after two years I still couldn't understand why we'd been singled out for such bad luck. Dad dead, Mum missing, an 'uncle' who hated me and a life so routine and monotonous that it felt more like a prison sentence than a childhood – it wasn't much of an existence.

Then I became angry for feeling so full of self-pity and the tears flowed once again. Yasir, who had been praying, using the words I had heard at Dad's funeral service, put his arm around my shoulders and gently steered me away from Dad's grave and towards the cemetery gate.

'Hey, little brother,' he said, 'don't upset yourself too much now. Your dad is with Allah, praised be His name. That's for sure. Come on, cheer up. Do you fancy a Coke? I do. This weather's something else, eh?'

I hadn't been much further than the compound and was keen to experience the centre of the village. I'd seen it from the van but hadn't yet walked around it. Yasir had been here many times before and would be a good guide. Not that there was much to see, but at least it wasn't Hawesmill.

We left the cemetery and turned into the main street. The shops were just opening again after the lunchtime shutdown, when the midday heat made it impossible for anyone to do anything effectively. There was a barber's, which seemed to be more of a place where men hung about and talked than had their hair cut or beards trimmed, and several fruit and vegetable shops. A row of small metal shacks sold hot food – meat with rice, chapatis and samosas – while others provided cold drinks, cigarettes and sweets. Yasir purchased two bottles of Coke from one of these and we sat in two orange plastic chairs and sipped our drinks while everyday life in Tajak passed us by.

The kebab man was oiling the massive iron bowl he used to fry chicken and lamb with a range of aromatic herbs and spices. A little further on, another stallholder was deep-frying sweet-corn. Across the road there was a tailor's shop, inside which stood a man being measured up for new *salwar kameez*. Cars, trucks, taxis, scooters and horse and carts all jostled for space on the narrow, dusty street. And everywhere there were men, men eating, talking, cooking, serving customers, driving vehicles, going to the mosque or loafing about watching the world go by, just like us. There wasn't a woman in sight.

'Oh, women don't get out much,' said Yasir airily when I asked him where they were. 'They've got stuff to do at home. Besides, it's not right for them to be wandering the streets on their own. If they want to go anywhere, they must have a male escort. Surely you know that?'

Of course I knew it. It was rare to see a woman out on her own in Hawesmill unless she was going to visit a friend, and even then she would more than likely take her husband, son or male cousin along as an escort. But I hadn't realized it applied here, too, and, by the looks of it, even more strictly. A woman out alone in Hawesmill might get a few people talking, but it wasn't a crime. Here, it seemed women were actively banned from the streets unless they were heavily escorted and fully veiled. Right on cue, a man walked past with a woman following several steps behind. She was silent; it was not done for a woman to speak to any man other than a family member, and even that was frowned upon in public.

In fact, life for women in Tajak seemed as boring and humdrum as it was for them in Hawesmill. I'd watched Alia and Little Fatima at work; their day started with a long sweeping of the veranda and garden with a broom made of twigs roughly fastened together. With this they'd gather up leaves and collect dung from various animals and throw it onto a big pile. Next they would water the orange trees and feed the chickens, goats and cow. There was no washing machine; Little Fatima, Alia and Farida pulled up buckets of water from the well and hand-scrubbed clothes which were later hung out in the garden and were dry within 15 minutes. The washing up from the previous day's meals was also done outside using well water. Later in the afternoon the women would grab a handful of animal dung from the big pile in the corner of the garden, mix it with some cut straw and mould it into the shape of a chapati. They'd fling this grim little pancake against the wall and leave it to dry. As afternoon turned into evening Alia or Little Fatima would peel the manure chapatis from the wall and use them as fuel in the *tandoor* for that evening's cooking.

When all that was done, though, the women were free to socialize, and I would often see Alia talking to her daughters under the grapevine or combing oil through their hair. Watching as she stroked their faces and made them laugh with her stories, I would always feel a pang of regret that I could not have the same mother-and-child relationship as they did.

Still, Alia was very kind to me and after a few days I felt very much part of the family. While Yasir was out on whatever business he had in Tajak, I would play around the garden with the younger kids. Occasionally we would venture out and fly kites in the surrounding fields under the supervision of Hussein or Ajmal. We didn't mix with the girls very much. It was allowed, as we were children, but I had the feeling that it wasn't entirely encouraged. However, one small girl aged about seven or eight attached herself to me and followed me everywhere I went. Her name was Parveen and she was Hussein's daughter. I was embarrassed at first and did my best to shake her off, but she stuck to me like glue. Surprisingly, none of the family members reprimanded us for being together. They even went as far as arranging a little party one night, at which we were guests of honour.

In fact the family seemed to have put some work into this gathering. I didn't take it very seriously, thinking it was some kind of variation on a game of 'princes and princesses'. Small sweet cakes were baked and Parveen and I were sat on two chairs at the head of a semi-circle of smiling relatives. Hussein appeared to be particularly pleased and kept patting me on the back and shaking my hand. Unfortunately Yasir was away from the compound that night, and while I could understand some Pashto, the excited family members were speaking far too quickly for me to pick up their conversation. Bemused, I went along with the fun and was glad to have played a part in keeping a small girl happy. Little did I realize how important this event actually was to all concerned.

Yasir's business had taken him all over the Attock district and now he had one more call to make before we were due to fly home. This was over the border in Afghanistan and, despite ongoing troubles in that country, it was decided that I should go with him, along with Grandma, Ajmal, Alia and their two children. The family had relatives there and Yasir's journey would be a good excuse to visit them.

I worried at first, having heard a bit about Afghanistan's long war with the Soviet Union, but Yasir assured me the area we were visiting was safe.

'Come on, Moham, even Grandma's not scared about coming,' he teased. 'You might never get a chance to go to Afghanistan again. And I'll tell you this – you're in more danger from other drivers on the mountain roads than the Russians!'

He wasn't kidding. We borrowed the old Transit van used to bring us from the airport and left Tajak very early one morning. As the sun rose we left the green fields of Pakistan behind and headed into far more mountainous and forbidding territory. The heat became more intense as the Ford started the long climb into the mountains which border the two countries. As we drove, Yasir told me stories of the invading armies who had used the path throughout history – the armies of Alexander the Great, Genghis Khan and the British Empire. 'They say every stone of this path is soaked in blood,' he said.

Undoubtedly it was harsh, cruel yet beautiful territory. The higher we got, the more the mountains came into view. Many of them were capped with snow. I'd never seen such breathtaking scenery and almost forgot the narrowness of the road and the stomach-turning hairpin bends the Ford had to negotiate. This wasn't made any easier by heavily-laden trucks hauling themselves up the mountainsides and hogging the road. We had to inch past several of them and at one stage we were brought to a complete halt by a truck that had broken down.

'OK,' shouted Ajmal, who was driving, 'everyone out!'

We climbed out and walked slowly past the truck driver, who simply shrugged and smiled, saying nothing. The truck was stranded on the nearside of the road, meaning that to get past it we would have to walk along the edge of the road which overlooked a drop. Yasir told me not to look down but to concentrate on the path ahead. Just as you do when someone tells you not to do something, I looked down momentarily and was horrified by what I saw. There was a sheer drop, possibly 1,000 feet, right to the valley floor, and not a thing to hold on to if I was to lose my footing. Alia held on tightly to her children and kept her head high. We all passed the truck without incident, but we held our breaths collectively when Ajmal inched the Transit past it with only a fraction of an inch or so to spare between him and instant death. Luckily, as a farmer he sometimes drove a truck himself and was used to getting out of tight spots.

Eventually the Afghan border loomed into view and after a quick check of papers we were in a foreign country and on the famous Khyber Pass. The village we were heading for was only 12 miles or so over the border, but after his fright with the broken-down truck Ajmal decided he needed a strong cup of tea. He pulled up at a roadside café and opened the bus's side door to let out his passengers. I was grateful for the stop, but not so happy when I saw who the café's customers were.

Sitting around three tables, smoking cigarettes, drinking tea and looking very relaxed, were a group of black-bearded men wearing black turbans and dark *salwar kameez*. Slung over the backs of their chairs was a collection of weaponry that would've shamed any military museum in the world. AK47s, pistols, bullet bandoliers and even a rocket launcher were openly on display.

I stared open-mouthed until Yasir nudged me fiercely, muttering under his breath in English. 'For God's sake don't gawp at them, you idiot! They're bad men, really bad men.'

One of them caught Yasir's accent and looked up with a grim expression. His eyes were all rimmed with kohl, giving him a weird and scary demeanour. I inched back in fear from the table.

'*Salaam*, brother,' said Yasir in Pashto, nodding in the man's direction, 'peace be upon you all.'

The man paused. '*Salaam*, brother,' he replied eventually, checking us out from head to toe before turning back to his comrades.

'Who are they, Yasir?' I asked as we queued for our tea.

Yasir pretended he hadn't heard me and appeared to be totally engrossed in a menu chalked on a blackboard. But I didn't need an answer. It was obvious they were *mujahideen* fighters enjoying a few days' R&R from conflicts far away in the north of Afghanistan. The guns and general appearance made me nervous, but secretly I was thrilled to see them. Sadeeq and Haani, my skiving friends from Hawesmill, had occasionally talked about the rebels who were beating the mighty Russians to a pulp, but I hadn't been that interested. Now I had something to contribute to that discussion – if Rafiq ever let me see my disgraced friends again.

The village where Grandma's relatives lived was smaller than Tajak and much scruffier. It wasn't rundown as such, just very basic. Individual houses were still contained in compounds, but the walls of these were lower and made almost entirely of sun-baked mud. To my shock, so too were the houses. I'd never been in anywhere so primitive. Although the houses in Tajak were basic, at least they were made of stone and brick. Their Afghan equivalents were mud right through and gave off an unpleasantly earthy, dirty smell.

The man of the house, Babur, was big, heavily bearded and armed, carrying an AK47 almost everywhere he went. This, I learned, wasn't because he was *mujahideen*; he carried it simply for self-protection against bandits and thugs, just like many men living in the area.

Though you wouldn't cross him, he was a softly-spoken man and was exceptionally pleased to see his visitors from over the border.

'Hi, Mohammed, how are you?' he said when he met me, politely shaking my hand. 'Welcome to Afghanistan – a bit different from England, hey?'

I salaamed him, unsure of how to reply. Afghanistan was completely different from Pakistan, and England was on another planet altogether. I'd seen TV pictures of famines in Africa, and the villages there looked exactly like this. I wasn't at all sure how we would spend the next few days, but Grandma seemed to be very pleased to see her relations. As the journey was more about her needs than anyone else's, I tried not to look as bored as I felt.

Because the village was made of mud, eating, sleeping and everything else was done within a thin film of dust. This also settled on the occupants. When we arrived we were met by two beautiful but incredibly grimy kids who looked as though they'd escaped from Victorian London. That said, I was struck by the greenness of their eyes, and could hardly believe that people in Afghanistan could look like that. I'd always thought that Asian people had uniformly brown eyes just like mine. Yasir told me later that some Pathans were descended from the Greek armies that had come rampaging through Afghanistan under Alexander the Great. Looking at these two children, with their pale skin and sea-green eyes, I could easily believe it.

The children's mother, Zakia, was an exceptionally shy woman who spent most of our four-day visit doing domestic chores and keeping out of the way of everyone, even Grandma and Alia. Compared to her way of life, the Tajak version looked like women's liberation. When she left the compound she was completely veiled, head to toe, leaving just a slit for her eyes. Although this is not an unfamiliar sight in Britain today, back then it was shocking and strange, even among my fellow Muslims. I felt sorry for her, trudging the dusty dirt-tracks by her house in the heat, covered in material as thick as a blanket. But that's how it was in Afghanistan.

Babur, like many of his neighbours, was a farmer of sorts, cultivating a dry patch of land to the back of his house. It wasn't a large patch by British farming standards, but it was enough to grow a decent-sized crop of sugar cane, which was being harvested at the time we arrived. Babur was pleased to see a few males arriving from Pakistan, as it meant extra hands in the field, and for a day or so we helped him gather in the harvest. Cutting the thick stems with a blunt billhook was back-breaking work, especially under the relentless Afghan sun, but there was the added bonus of being able to chew the sweet innards of the cane once the thick outer shell had been broken off and the whole thing chopped into bite-sized pieces. Once it was chewed to a pulp, the remaining cane was simply spat onto the ground. It wasn't quite as tasty as an Everton mint, but it was certainly sweet and it gave you enough glucose to keep going through a long hot day's work in the field.

Babur was evidently pleased with our efforts, so at the end of the afternoon's cutting he took Yasir, Ajmal and me into the village for a drink. We walked the half-mile or so, passing dreary mud-houses that had lethal-looking electrical wiring draped all over them and slung low across the streets. We stopped at a roadside café where the usual line-up of men was sitting, smoking and taking tea. We expected a refreshing glass of the same, but Babur decided to push the boat out and we got a bottle of Fanta each. He watched, delighted, as we sipped at it and kept asking if we were enjoying it. We were honoured guests and a bottle of Fanta was a way of conferring that status on us.

There was precious little else in the way of luxury in Afghanistan. I feel terrible saying this, as Babur and his wife looked after us as best they could, but the food was terrible, the worst I've ever tasted. Knives and forks were non-existent (although we didn't use them in Pakistan, to be fair) and everything cooked was shared communally. A grubby drinking bowl containing some kind of flavoured filthy water was passed between us all before the meal started. The food itself was made up of chewed, highly seasoned lumps of meat that contained more fat, bone and gristle than anything else, and chewing on these for what seemed like 20 minutes or more at a time was pure torture. It came with a thick yellow chapati made from ground corn, which at least helped to disguise the flavour of the meat. We were, of course, expected to show our gratitude for the meal, and there were murmurs of content from all around the room. I wondered how many of those were genuine; I know mine certainly weren't.

After the cane-cutting there was very little for us to do. Wandering off alone wasn't an option, as we'd been warned about kidnappers, bandits and rogue *mujahideen* who would fire off AK47 rounds at anything that moved, including pale-skinned visitors from across the border. I spent a lot of time in the shade of a plane tree which Babur had planted himself some years previously, playing with the green-eyed children. Their only toy was an old bicycle wheel that had a revolving metal bar fastened to its rim. Holding this, they would spin the wheel round and chase after it once it had gathered speed. They played like this for hours and never seemed to be bored. I watched them and wondered if they were happy. They would have been amazed to see what was available for children in the West, and yet I was denied access to all that almost as comprehensively as these little ones were, and I lived there. They knew nothing about the wider world and didn't seem to mind. I was well aware of what lay beyond Hawesmill and it troubled me to think that I would never get to grips with it – especially if Rafiq had his way.

Thankfully we didn't stay too long in Afghanistan. The heat made Grandma quite tired and after four days she was ready to go home. After a final yet no less disgusting feast of fatty meat we said our goodbyes to Babur, his silent wife and their two children and set off towards the border with Pakistan. I'd been interested to see the country but had very little desire to spend any more time in such a desolate, harsh and fundamentalist place.

Within a few hours we were back in Tajak, and this time we hadn't almost gone down a ravine or been scrutinized by freedom fighters. I was very pleased to see the compound again, but not quite as happy to see that Imran, Rafiq's brooding, intense brother, had made himself at home in Little Fatima's house and seemed to be there to stay.

From what I could gather, Imran had various jobs and during my time in Pakistan had been away on a construction site in Lahore, labouring and doing general handyman work. The contract had finished and he was now back with his wife, Little Fatima's daughter, and their three children in the compound. I knew he was building his own house somewhere on the other side of Tajak but from what I heard the work was nowhere near finished. In the meantime he was enjoying all the creature comforts of home without paying too much towards the cost. He and Rafiq were birds of a feather in that respect.

In the days following our return I noticed Imran and Yasir speaking frequently together and taking walks outside the compound. A couple of times I asked if I could go with them; instinctively I felt that Imran didn't like me, but somehow I thought that if he got to know me better he would change his opinion. But every time I asked, the answer was a definite 'no'. Yasir looked slightly uncomfortable about this, but Imran was older and this was his territory. His word was law.

Yasir and Imran were both married to Little Fatima's daughters, so there was a strong family connection between the two men and I assumed they were talking family business. In my experience Pakistani men didn't talk about much else other than business, the weather and the general state of life at home and in their adopted country. I imagined that Yasir was just trying to straighten out a few things before we went home. There could be no other reason for their regular little huddles under the vine or walks into the village.

At last the day of our return home finally arrived. In the morning, Yasir insisted I visit Dad's grave once more.

'It's the done thing, Mohammed,' he said, peering at me. After weeks in sunglasses, he had his usual big black-framed spectacles on again and looked like a nerdy student once more instead of the high-flying international business traveller he considered himself to be.

'Can't we just pack and go, Yasir?' I said. 'I did all that grave-yard stuff when I got here. Dad knows I love him and that I came to see him. What else can I say?'

'You can say that you are making your peace with him,' Yasir replied gravely, 'and that you promise to be a good boy and do your best.'

'I've promised that a thousand times, but no one ever bloody listens,' I thought. But I didn't want to seem cheeky, so I said nothing and nodded.

So, for the last time, we strolled through Tajak, nodding to the barber, the tailor and the kebab-maker. They all knew who we were, but it didn't stop them staring as hard as they had done when we had arrived. At least now they smiled and waved too, calling out to us as we walked by.

'People are so friendly here,' Yasir said, 'not like in England. Doesn't it make you want to stay forever?'

'No way!' I said quickly. 'It's OK, but it's dead boring. At least in England you've got …'

'Nice white girls?' he interrupted.

'No, I wasn't gonna say that. In England you've got people you know and stuff to do. People to talk to.'

'You can talk to people here.'

'But not in English. It's … home. Sort of. But it doesn't feel like that. It's too foreign.'

Yasir laughed. 'I know what you mean, little brother. I couldn't live here, to be honest. I've been in England since I was a kid. I couldn't leave it now.'

'Me neither,' I said, pleased that Yasir was on my side.

We reached the graveyard and stood by Dad's grave. I felt it might be the last time I would ever stand in this spot and I thanked God that Dad had given me life. The old feelings of anger and regret rose to the surface again, but this time I put them aside. I knew I'd done my duty as a Muslim and I hadn't got into trouble for a single thing while I'd been away. I'd honoured Dad's memory and he would be proud of me. I had nothing to feel guilty about. I cried, of course, because I didn't want to leave Dad lying in the cracked sun-baked earth forever. But it was time to go.

Palms upward, I said my final prayers and a last goodbye to Dad before turning away and walking back towards the compound with Yasir. As it came into view I could see a little knot of relatives gathered by the old Ford minibus that would take us to Islamabad. At last I was going home.

Chapter Nine

The group that gathered for our farewell to Pakistan wasn't as large as the one that had greeted us a few weeks before. Hussein and Ajmal were both working and several others were absent for various reasons. Little Fatima was there, along with her daughter Farida, the lively, pig-tailed young woman who had been so interested to hear about England when I had arrived. I hadn't seen much of her since that day. I knew she'd been sent to see some elderly relatives for a few weeks. When she'd come back she'd seemed subdued and unwilling to talk. That had been fine with me; I didn't want yet another relative reminding me that I must behave like a good Muslim boy.

Naturally, Aunty Alia was there to see us off. As I threw my bag into the old Ford that had brought us to Tajak and taken us to Afghanistan, she hugged me and started crying.

'It's been lovely having you, Mohammed,' she sniffed. 'Do take care. You're becoming a nice young man. I'm proud of you.'

'Thanks, aunty,' I said. 'I'll write to you when I get home. I won't forget you.'

She pulled her scarf across her face and turned away. I was surprised at how upset she was. We had become close over the past weeks, but this felt more like a farewell to a beloved son than to a nephew she hardly knew. Embarrassed, I took her hand and squeezed it before getting into the Ford.

Yasir said his own round of goodbyes and got in next to me. A male cousin was also coming along for the ride. I hadn't seen much of him, as he was about 16 and already working long hours in the fields. I guessed this journey to Islamabad was the equivalent of a day's holiday for him.

Then the driver's door opened and in slid Imran, my not-uncle, brother of the dreaded Rafiq. He and Yasir exchanged glances, then Imran turned the key and revved the old engine hard to kick some life into it. This was strange. He'd had nothing to do with me while we'd been visiting and yet here he was driving us back to the airport. He and Yasir seemed close, but he wasn't the sort of guy who'd do anything for anyone, even his closest buddies. A chill crept up my spine as we lurched off, the van's wheels spinning dust into the faces of those waving us goodbye. Aunty Alia had already gone inside.

Passing through Tajak, we were chased by smiling local kids who knew we were going home. No doubt they expected us to throw them a few unwanted rupees out of the window, and Yasir didn't disappoint them.

'You shouldn't give them anything,' said Imran, 'they're just little beggars.'

'Oh come on, Imran,' said Yasir, 'they're only kids. They expect it.'

Imran said nothing, just put his foot down a touch harder so he could shake off the excited children. I tried to ignore his obvious bad mood and instead settled back for a sleep. I'd been up earlier than usual that morning and suddenly felt tired. The experiences I'd had in the last few weeks crammed into my head – getting to know the village shopkeepers, sleeping out under the stars, spending time with relatives, travelling to Afghanistan. It was all interesting stuff. I hoped it would keep me sane in the weeks and months ahead, as I endured life at home with Abida and Rafiq. I was looking forward to getting back to England, but not to spending endless boring days hanging around the streets of Hawesmill trying not to get into trouble. On the whole I'd enjoyed Pakistan, though I didn't want to live there. I knew too much about Western ways to ever fit in properly.

I woke up with a start just before we reached Islamabad airport. I'd been leaning on Yasir's shoulder for most of the journey and he looked relieved that I was no longer slobbering down his jacket sleeves.

Imran swung the Ford into the airport and almost immediately Yasir stepped out, grabbed his suitcase from the seat behind him and strode towards the sign marked 'Departures'.

'Hang on!' I shouted. 'Wait for me!'

I ran round to the back of the vehicle and opened the door. I hauled my bag out and cradled it with two hands. But just as I was about to set off running after Yasir, my 16-year-old cousin stepped out in front of me.

'Move over, you idiot, I'm in a rush!' I shouted.

The youth just stood there, his arms folded and his mouth creased into a tight zip. He was obviously blocking my way. I tried to push past him, but he was a strapping village lad, built like an ox. I called out to Yasir, but although he was still well within hearing distance he didn't turn round. Then I felt a strong bony hand clutch my shoulder.

'You aren't going anywhere, son. Get back in the van.'

I turned to face a snarling Imran. I tried to pull away from him, but his grip was too strong. He pushed me against the van door and my bag fell on the ground.

Again I screamed for Yasir, but he either hadn't heard or was taking no notice whatsoever.

'Get back in the van, you little bastarrd!'

Imran pronounced the word just like his evil brother and my eyes widened in horror. What the hell was he doing? Why had Yasir just left me like this? I couldn't believe what was happening.

'Let me go! Let me go! I'm not going anywhere with you! Get off me!'

I kicked and struggled and shoved and bit, but it was hopeless. Imran and the youth bundled me back into the van and slammed the door, then locked it from the outside. Quickly Imran slid into the driver's seat and gunned the engine, then slammed the van into first gear and sped out of Islamabad airport as if every cop in Pakistan was on his tail. Which, unfortunately for me, they weren't.

I was still shouting, but Imran took no notice at all. Every time I yelled, the youth gave me a dig in the side with his elbow, though, accompanied by a look that promised a beating if I carried on. After ten miles or so I gave up and slumped back in my seat, resigned to whatever fate they had in store for me. But what was it? I thought I'd behaved very well in Pakistan. I hadn't upset anyone or missed mosque. I'd been helpful around the compound and I'd got on well with my relatives, particularly Alia. And as for Yasir – what the fuck was he playing at? He'd completely abandoned me, clearing off without so much as a backwards glance.

Imran was really flooring the vehicle now, as if he was desperate to get somewhere he knew I didn't want to be. I was helpless; I'd been tricked and betrayed, and I'd no idea what the hell was going to happen to me when this maniac finally stopped driving. Would he abandon me by the road? Would he take me to some old building and shoot me like a dog? I tried to keep the rising panic down, but it was no good, and within seconds my sobs were drowning out the overworked diesel engine.

'Shut up,' Imran hissed, 'or you'll get what you really deserve.'

'Where are you taking me?' I pleaded. 'I want to go back to England.'

Imran turned round and gave me the strangest, ugliest grin I'd ever seen. Boy, did he look like his brother sometimes.

'You've been very bad, Mohammed, very bad indeed. That's what I hear. So we need to sort that out, don't we, little boy?'

'I dunno what you mean …'

'Wait and see,' he said, 'wait and see.'

I didn't want to wait and see. I wanted to go home. But we seemed to be heading straight back to Tajak. The thought of spending a few more weeks there while Imran 'sorted out' my behaviour made me feel sick. Suddenly Hawesmill and its wet greasy streets seemed very appealing indeed. I'd actually missed proper Lancashire rain while I'd been away and was looking forward to splashing through puddles in my cheap trainers on the way home from mosque. There didn't seem to be much chance of that now. In frustration I banged my fist against the door of the van and, for my pains, got another fierce dig in the ribs.

The Ford finally turned off the main road and, as I expected, headed down the dirt road that led to Tajak. Once again, the kids in the main street ran behind the van, laughing and shouting. Imran opened the window and told them to piss off. They laughed at him and hurled small stones against the bodywork. Imran screeched to a halt and the kids cleared off like scattering mice. He'd no chance of catching them and he knew it, so he carried on down the main street and pulled up against the wall of the compound.

I was relieved by this. Surely Alia would be out any moment, demanding to know why I'd missed my flight. She'd sort it out and I would be home very quickly.

Imran came round the side of the van, opened the passenger door and dragged me out by the hair. At the same time my cousin put me in an arm-lock and the pair of them shoved me through the open gate and into the compound. I felt as though I was under arrest and was sure that if Alia saw how they were treating me she would stop them in their tracks. But there was no Alia there, or Little Fatima, Hussein, Ajmal or Farida. The place was deserted. Even the animals in the courtyard seemed subdued.

I was pulled into Little Fatima's house and forced upstairs into a room I'd never been in before. Imran quickly shut the heavy wooden door and locked it from the outside. I shouted a couple of times, but it was pointless. The only window was meshed and barred and faced outwards. If anyone could hear me, they were taking no notice.

There was a single bed in one corner with a rough blanket thrown over it. I sat down on it, feeling distraught and bewildered. I tried to recall anything I'd done to upset Imran, or anyone else, and not a single thing came to mind. In my mind's eye I saw Imran's face grinning from the driver's seat of the van, and it seemed to fuse into Rafiq's. The pair were horribly entwined, and I began to wonder whether this latest attempt at discipline had, in fact, originated in Hawesmill, not Tajak.

Locked in a small room, a virtual prisoner far from home, I cried myself to sleep that night. My dreams were tormented by visions of what had happened so unexpectedly that day. Several times I shouted out loud and woke myself up. Then, at some point in the night, the key turned very gently in the lock and in came Alia. I opened my eyes to see her sitting beside me on the bed, holding my hand and cooling me with a large raffia fan. It seemed like another dream, but her touch felt real enough.

'Aunty Alia, what's happening? Why am I still here? I want to go home. Can you tell me what's happening?'

'Oh, Mohammed ...' she began. Then the door was pushed open and a tall thin shadow filled the frame. It was Imran. He spoke quickly and harshly to Alia in Punjabi, a language I had no knowledge of, and she immediately got up and left without saying another word.

Imran banged the door shut and locked it. Exhausted, I fell asleep again.

When dawn came, so did Imran and my cousin. Again, no one else was around. Only a pair of stray dogs that usually hung around the compound wall waiting for food scraps witnessed two figures pushing a sleepy young teenager into the back of a car and driving off.

This time, though, we didn't go very far. Journey's end was a *baytuk*, a café in the middle of Tajak. As we arrived, three men I'd never seen before were waiting there. They surrounded me and I was bundled out of the car and into the *baytuk*. One of them had a length of plastic rope. Once inside, I was pushed to the floor and my arms and legs tied together.

I could barely breathe with fear. I was certainly too frightened to speak. I'd seen bits on the telly about kidnappings and they always looked like this: one victim, several men and a quiet time of day. The snippet usually ended with the police lifting a body out of the boot of a car or, worse still, the body not being found at all. I wanted to cry, but was scared that if I did, I would be tortured or killed.

After 10 minutes of chatting, two of the strange men lifted me bodily out of the *baytuk* and into a van. I was laid along the back seat and a rice bag full of what felt like clothes was placed on top of me. Seatbelts didn't exist in Pakistan – most drivers saw them as cowardly – so I was left to the mercy of Imran's driving as he bumped and rolled his way through Tajak and out onto the main road.

The men had lashed me very tightly and if I tried to move the plastic rope cut and burned my wrists. My face was jammed against a warm and dirty leatherette seat and trying to twist my neck away to get some air was pointless. All the windows were shut and every other occupant of the vehicle was chain-smoking. It didn't seem to bother them at all that the atmosphere was stifling. They made jokes about me and laughed.

At one stage I asked them where I was going.

'It's a surprise, Mohammed,' replied Imran. 'I think you'll like it. You'll learn a lot. And not a white girl in sight!'

They all laughed again. So the story about my innocent encounters with a trio of giggling English girls had reached as far as here. No doubt it had been hugely exaggerated along the way. Someone – and I could guess who – had decided that I hadn't been punished hard enough. Whatever they had in store for me now was designed to teach me a lesson I would never forget.

After almost two hours I pleaded with Imran to let me sit up. The pins and needles in my hands and feet were excruciating and my face was unbelievably sweaty from the seat. He thought about it for a few seconds, then ordered one of the men to pull me up.

Aching and dehydrated, I slowly straightened my back and stared out of the window. I had no idea where we were and the landscape gave away few clues. We were in a very barren area, with no trees or cultivated fields or signs of human life. You could call it a desert, but that might be stretching it a bit far. Even so, it was a lifeless and inhospitable-looking place, surrounded by high mountains. I prayed silently that I was not going to be abandoned here.

After 20 minutes we turned off the highway and began to climb a hill, twisting and turning around a variety of hairpin bends. I wondered if we were back in Afghanistan, or somewhere close to the border. Though as we hadn't stopped and been accosted by border guards I assumed we were still somewhere in Pakistan. But where?

As we approached the top of the hill we came across the strangest sight: either side of the dirt road was strewn with huge boulders and perched on these were around half-a-dozen young lads, all clad in white *salwar kameez* and clutching copies of the Qur'an tightly to their chests. As they prayed they rocked backwards and forwards, so much so that some looked as though they were about to fall off. In different circumstances it might've looked funny.

As we neared a huge building surrounded by a high wall, with an imposing set of thick wooden gates guarding its entrance, I began to get an inkling of where we were. The building was topped with a big green dome, and a tall minaret by its side reached up high towards heaven. As we approached, the gates were opened, and just before we went through them

I caught a glimpse of a sign in Arabic fixed to the wall, I could just make out the word 'school'. And not just any old school either, as I would find out.

The van pulled up a few yards inside the walls of the compound, kicking up dust as the wheels ground to a sudden halt. The square was very large – it had to be to accommodate the mosque standing right in the centre, the biggest I'd ever seen. I'd been used to mosques created from rundown terrace houses in Hawesmill, and although the one in Tajak was substantial enough, it had nothing on this place. Young men and boys were milling outside its doors, which were ornately decorated within strict Islamic rules, i.e. no representations of living creatures, including humans.

Imran opened the side door of the van and pulled me out. One of the men accompanying us pulled out a short knife and cut the rope from my hands and feet then threw the rice sack at me. I opened it and saw my clothes lying in a jumbled heap at the bottom.

A man approached us from the other side of the courtyard. He wore white and had a long grey beard. He looked vaguely Chinese and I wondered how he'd become a Muslim. He shook hands with Imran then embraced him like a long-lost friend.

Imran pointed to me then came over and pulled me towards the man. 'He's all yours now, brother,' he said. 'He's been a very bad lad. I know that you will make a very good Muslim out of him.'

Then he turned to me.

'Get out of my sight,' he muttered. 'I don't want to see you again until you've learned to behave. Understand?'

I nodded dumbly, not understanding at all. Without another word, not even a goodbye, Imran and his buddies got back into the car and drove off. They didn't even stop for tea, which is obligatory when you're visiting someone in those parts. To refuse is exceptionally rude, but Imran must've been so relieved to get rid of me that he didn't care what anyone said about him.

I watched the vehicle drive through the open gates, which slammed shut the moment it had gone. A huge lump appeared in my throat and I squeezed my eyes tightly shut to stop the tears from falling. I'd been in some situations in my 13 years of life, but I'd never felt so isolated and frightened as I did at that moment. I stood there, the rice sack at my feet, totally alone, abandoned and unwanted. The walls of the compound looked forbiddingly high, especially to a young boy. Beyond those walls was a desert – no place to escape to. The sun beat mercilessly down, exposing me in its full glare. There was no shade, no protection, nowhere to hide. I scraped my sandal on the ground, as an animal might do on strange territory. Under the dust there was nothing but stony yellow earth. Ahead, a few boys shuffled past, murmuring to themselves in languages I didn't understand. No one even bothered to look in my direction. What chance was there of anyone speaking English here? How could I say that I was terrified and wanted to go home? Who would protect me against whatever fate had in store here? If someone told me that I'd died and this was hell, I would've believed them. This was truly hell on Earth.

The Chinese-looking man said something to me that I didn't understand, then beckoned to me. Not knowing what else to do, I followed him into a kind of cloister within the shadow of the walls. We passed several closed doors until we came to one that was slightly ajar. The man pushed it open and we went into a dingy room with a table at one end with a large cooking pot placed on it. The man produced a rough clay bowl and heaped out a spoon of what looked like lentil dhal into it, then offered it me. The dhal was stone cold, but it was the first food I'd had in hours and I ate it gratefully, along with a chapati he passed me.

When I had finished, he summoned me with the same finger gesture as before and I walked with him back across the court-yard to a large hall at the side of the mosque. Boys were sprawled like ants all over its grey marble floor. Some were praying, others reading the Qur'an silently. A few groups were sitting around chatting. It was still relatively early and the sight of people sitting around, plus the food that had just hit my stomach, formed a wave of tiredness that suddenly washed over me.

The man led me through the hall and into a dark ante-room that was filled with boys asleep on rush mats. 'Lie down, go asleep,' he commanded in broken Pashto. 'I'll be back for you later.'

Then he left.

I found a spare rush mat and lay down, trying not to return the hostile glances of boys woken up by me stumbling across the floor to a quiet corner of the room. I didn't care what they thought. I was too weary to be bothered and within a few minutes I was sound asleep.

I don't know how long I lay there, but it must have been some hours because when I woke up – or, rather, was woken up by a sandalled foot gently kicking me in the ribs – I knew instinctively that it was dark outside. The Chinese guy was telling me to get up and join evening prayers. The room was deserted and I was the last to leave. What a great impression I was making already ...

The man led me to an ablutions room which was far more basic than anything I'd encountered in Hawesmill. There was simply a bucket of water with a funnel by its side. The man indicated that I should complete the ritual wash – *wudu* – before prayers. At least I knew how to do that, though I winced when I saw the colour of the water. Quite a few dirty bodies had already used the bucket before me. Quickly I did what was necessary and followed the man into the prayer hall.

It was cavernous, the biggest I'd ever seen. There must have been 300 or 400 men and boys in there, all kneeling and listening to the imam. As is usual in mosques across the world, the elders were at the front and the youngest at the back. The elders looked a formidable bunch. They were all heavily bearded and wore dark robes and turbans. The *adhan*, or call to prayer, had already taken place and I'd obviously missed it. I scuttled in between a row of youths towards the back and muttered what prayers I understood amid wave after wave of Arabic coming from the front.

'*Ash-had al-la ilāha illa llah, ash-hadu anna Muhammadan-rasūlu llāh!*' ('I testify that there is no God except Allah, I testify that Muhammad is a Messenger of Allah!')

It was the best I could do under the circumstances, and I still didn't really know what the circumstances were. I felt like not praying at all; I couldn't believe it was God's will that I should be dumped in this place for the sake of one little misdemeanour. Again I searched my mind for anything I might have done to offend anyone while in Pakistan, and again I drew a blank.

Down we went, on our knees, praying hard to God to forgive us for our sins as the imam called out the verses. As usual I copied everyone else's movements, and I must've done OK that evening, despite everything, as I didn't get the usual expressions of irritation and annoyance from my neighbours in prayer. Or maybe it was because there were so many people around that I just blended into the background.

Feeling confident, I asked my nearest neighbour in Pashto where we were. He looked at me with a puzzled expression and continued praying. But the lad kneeling on the other side of him had heard me. After a few minutes there was a pause in the prayer ceremony and he leaned round the back of his neighbour.

'You're new, aren't you?'

It was about the worst Pashto I'd ever heard, and I could hardly understand it, but I got the gist. I nodded in response.

'Where am I?' I asked.

'Welcome to Darul Uloom Haqqania,' he said, smiling.

'Uh?'

'This is a madrassa,' he said, 'an Islamic school. You must have heard of this place?'

I shook my head. 'I was just brought here,' I said. 'I didn't want to come. And I dunno where I am.'

The lad smiled again, trying hard to contain his laughter. 'Then you must have been a very naughty boy,' he said. 'A very naughty boy indeed ...'

Chapter Ten

After prayers we trooped back to the sleeping quarters. The passageway was now lit by torches and was far bigger than I'd originally thought. It was more like a dormitory, though without any beds, just rugs and blankets scattered across the stone floor. The babble of many different languages filled the narrow corridor as dozens of boys, released from the formality of evening prayers, chattered away. There were Punjabi and Pashto speakers, Uzbeks and Kazakhs, Saudis and Yemenis – the madrassa appeared to cater for boys right across the Muslim world. Although I didn't know it then, this was the school of choice for many influential – and soon-to-be notorious – families.

I sat with my back to the wall, feeling very much the new boy. I would've been amazed to find another English boy in this place. I listened hard, but I couldn't hear any trace of a familiar accent, except for Pashto speakers.

After 10 minutes or so of socializing, the boys gathered into a kind of crocodile, the biggest and oldest at the front and the very youngest, at about 10 or 11, at the bottom. I stood up, rooted inside the rice bag Imran had thrown at me and picked out my grimy grey woollen shawl. Then I placed myself in the queue roughly where I thought would be right for my age.

No sooner was I in the queue than I was out again – a shove in the back and a string of angry-sounding words in a language I didn't understand saw to that. I stared at the boy who'd pushed me. Was he going to follow it up with a smack on the nose? He didn't. Instead, he jerked his thumb towards the back of the queue. Meekly I followed it, trying to ignore the whispers and the jeers as I took my place with the youngest boys at the back. Obviously, it wasn't a pecking order based on age after all – or at least that's what I thought. Maybe I was being singled out because I was British. But how would I know unless someone told me?

The crocodile set off in the direction of the communal kitchen, the place I'd been taken to previously by the Chinese man. He was nowhere to be seen now. At the head of a long table stood a grey-bearded elder. He had a solemn expression and was flanked by two much older students.

One by one we lined up. From a huge cooking pot we were given a portion of curry and a chapati. The portions were tiny and I wondered how I'd get through the night on what amounted to not much more than a soup spoonful. Unlike Oliver Twist, I wasn't going to ask for more. The expression on the elder's face as he slapped the gluey curry into the wooden bowl was enough to make me realize it wouldn't be a helpful request.

The boys didn't sit down at the table to eat. They either lapped up the curry where they stood or wandered off into the courtyard to perch under the veranda. I noticed how they divided into little sub-groups; I couldn't imagine myself ever being part of such a group, or fitting into this place at all. Awkwardly I mooched around the courtyard, trying not to look like the new boy. Apart from a brief period at primary, I'd never attended school. I had no idea of how you 'got in' with other people. I also had no idea that if you looked like an outcast it was very likely you'd be treated like one. In the weeks and months that followed, I would learn that the hard way.

Dinner over, we filed back to the dormitory. Once we'd settled underneath our blankets, the torches were blown out. The darkness in that chamber, and all around the madrassa, was total. Even night-time in Tajak was illuminated by street lights, car headlights and lanterns. Out here, in the middle of God-knows-where, the blackness was as deep as the ocean. I shut my eyes and tried to understand what had happened to me. Yesterday I was on my way home to England; tonight I was a prisoner in a place that appeared to have no means of escape. And for what reason?

As ever, I turned to the question of my mum. Why had she left us and what would've happened if she hadn't? I pictured a typical English front room, like the ones I'd been told about by the white girls in Hawesmill. There was a mum and a dad, watching the telly or reading the newspaper, while the kids played quietly on the floor. There were no rows, no disruption, no imported uncles and no demands of different cultures to deal with. Life was comfortable, safe and easy. At the heart of this family I placed my own mum, content with what she had. But I had a feeling that if she was still alive, her life must be very different from the picture I'd imagined. Did she wonder where we were? Did she care? Had she other children now and did she love them more than us? I began to cry quietly, even as sleep blanketed me as heavily as snowfall.

The shattering call of the muezzin making the call to prayer from the top of the minaret jerked me awake. I'd been used to this in Tajak, but never at such close quarters. The minaret loomed over us like a huge chimney and the loudspeaker sounded as though it was located right next to my ear. It only felt like five minutes since I'd fallen asleep, but it was already time for morning prayers.

In Tajak it was customary for the men of the village to go to mosque before starting work. I'd tag along with Ajmal, Hussein and Yasir and anyone else they met on the way, before returning home to a nice breakfast prepared by Aunty Alia. Going to mosque, both in Tajak and Hawesmill, was such an inbuilt part of my life that I took it completely for granted. That doesn't mean I was always keen to go, but by and large I was a dutiful young Muslim – despite what Rafiq thought – and I tried my best to fit in with the demands of the religion, even though I often didn't understand what was going on.

Now once again I followed the herd as we walked into the mosque and lined up on the prayer mats. I copied the sitting and kneeling actions of those nearest to me, feeling slightly smug that once again I'd got away with not quite knowing how to behave in this particular situation. I don't know why I had a blind spot about the prayer ceremony; it was something I could have and should have easily overcome, but a part of my brain didn't connect with the words and actions, and no matter how hard I tried, the formalities of the ceremony wouldn't stick. Even today I read the Qur'an in English only – the Arabic version is still a mystery to me.

The breakfast that followed was the remnants of the previous evening's curry, and the portions were even more meagre. No wonder so many of the boys were thin. They ate quickly, then walked off towards a set of doors on the other side of the compound. Bolting down my curry, I hurried to catch the stragglers, and as I did so one of the more senior boys glared at me and said something in Arabic that I didn't catch.

'Huh?' I said, sounding stupid.

'He's telling you that it is the unbelievers who are late into class,' said a lad behind me in Pashto. 'Come on, hurry up or you'll get it.'

By this time the older boy had produced a stick and was swishing it around menacingly. I ran across the courtyard and in through a door. The boys were filing into rows of low benches. Each was holding a copy of the Qur'an that had been given to him at the door. At the front of the room was a blackboard with several verses chalked in Arabic on it.

I took my place, half-kneeling, half-squatting on the bench, and started to flick through the Holy Book. Two or three older boys stood in the gap between the benches and the wall, watching intently as we settled down. I could feel my heart rising to my throat as I looked blankly at the script on the pages. Judging by the complete lack of any other textbooks or pictures on the walls, there was only one subject on the curriculum – Islam.

My mood dropped further when the door opened and in walked a cleric, heavily bearded and dressed entirely in black. Without so much as a glance at us he took his place at the head of the class and opened his copy of the Qur'an. He said something in Arabic and the boys flicked through their books to the correct page. My eyes darted left and right, trying to catch a glimpse of the page I should be on. But even the page numbers were in Arabic. I had no chance, and sat miserable and sweating as the cleric pointed a short stick at a lad towards the front, commanding him to begin the recitation.

The boy spoke and the whole class – except one – followed, their fingers tracing the script as the words tumbled out. Occasionally the lad stumbled over something and in response the cleric tapped his stick against his desk. The patrolling older boys moved towards him, crowding him menacingly as he tried again to get it right. Meanwhile, the rest of the class mumbled along at the same time. I'd assumed it was rude to speak out loud in such a situation, but I quickly realized that not only did you have to look as if you knew the Holy Book back to front, you had to be seen and heard to know it. If you were silent, it meant other thoughts were occupying your mind – sinful thoughts, no doubt. So I jabbered nonsensically, saying anything that came into my head that sounded vaguely Arabic. The boys to my immediate left and right looked at me with raised eyebrows but said nothing. If I kept my head down and looked as though I knew what I was doing, I might just get away with it.

The hours went by and the monotonous drone of one reader after another, combined with the increasing temperature outside, caused my eyelids to droop several times. I wasn't the only one either; some of the younger boys were also flagging, but were pulled up swiftly by their patrolling elders. I didn't want to get caught and beaten. I breathed deeply and forced myself to concentrate on the unfathomable script on the page. I dreaded catching the teacher's eye in case he asked me to read or, worse still, recite. As almost all the boys had had a turn, I knew the spotlight was bound to fall on me sooner or later.

A young boy, no more than 10 years old, began confidently enough but started to falter after a couple of minutes. The prefects sauntered over to the back of the class, hovering over him as he stuttered his way through the verse.

After another 30 seconds or so, the teacher could take no more. 'Stop!' he commanded. 'Come out to the front.'

The lad reluctantly pulled himself up from the bench and began a slow walk towards the teacher. It didn't last long. One of the prefects grabbed him by the hair and propelled him forwards. He cried out and received a whack on the back of the leg for doing so. I could feel the rush of air from the swish of the cane. My bowels turned to water. The imams and teachers had been strict at the mosque in Hawesmill, but they had been nothing compared to this.

The lad was crying and shaking as he stood in front of the teacher, who seemed to take delight in his fear. He stood up and very deliberately pinched the tops of the boy's ears, pulling him upwards by them until he was practically on tiptoes. The lad cried out, then became scarily quiet as he took his punishment. He must have known that any screaming would have meant an even more severe penalty.

I couldn't believe what I was seeing and turned to my neighbours on the bench. They weren't even looking up, just continuing to read as though this was the most normal thing in the world. Terrified, I looked towards the end of the bench and caught the eye of the boy who had told me where I was on the night of my arrival. With a quick hand gesture he told me to look downwards and not to stare. I did as I was told, trying not to glance up at the boy, who was by now almost off his feet.

Then the teacher let go and the boy thudded to the ground and remained motionless. The teacher stepped over him, shaking his stick. This time he spoke in Pashto.

'I've told you all before and I will tell you again: anyone unable to read the Holy Book – at whatever age – will be punished. If they continue to show disrespect to God, there will be worse to come. Understand?'

We nodded mutely. I stared at my feet, hoping and praying that I wouldn't be selected to read. But as the boy picked himself up off the floor and limped back to his seat, the teacher decided to read the Holy Book himself until the end of the lesson. Then the class was dismissed and from there we went straight into the mosque for a good hour of prayer and sermons before we were allowed something to eat. After that it was back to the classroom for the afternoon session.

Somehow I ended up towards the front of the class. I'd again made the mistake of dawdling back after the meal and in the scrum for places at the back of the class had lost out big time. I was completely within the teacher's sight-line. As he walked in, black robes swishing on the concrete floor, a feeling of dread rose within me. 'Oh God,' I said to myself, half-praying, half-pleading, 'I've got to get out of this place. I have to go! God, please help me …'

This was only the first full day of my time at Haqqania and already I was very stressed. If this was what it was going to be like day in day out forever, I knew I'd go mad. One way or another I had to leave this place. A powerful, almost unstoppable feeling rose up that threatened to overwhelm me. I had to force myself to stay seated and not suddenly bolt for the door.

Silence enveloped the room as the teacher took his place. He commanded a kid to read and sat back, closing his eyes in deep concentration. This went on for several minutes and not once did the teacher open his eyes. He began to sway back and forth and a few seconds later his head drooped. Never mind deep religious concentration – the silly bugger was asleep.

I wasn't the only one to have noticed. Around me, boys began to nudge each other and gesture with their eyes towards the front. There was shuffling and stifled giggles. A couple of lads to the left of me started playfully punching each other in the sides. The prefects hadn't yet arrived back from lunch and we were doing what kids the world over do when no one appears to be in control – messing about and having a laugh.

Then someone pushed someone else off their bench and the commotion woke the teacher. Immediately the class snapped to attention, but not being very schooled in the ways of school, I was leaning back casually on my bench when his eyes opened and he caught me red-handed. He held my gaze for a few seconds, perhaps weighing up whether it was worth hauling me out. With hindsight I wish he had done so, for what was to come was far worse.

He flicked through his copy of the Qur'an and said something to me in Arabic. I turned to the lad on my left, who muttered something to the teacher.

'What do you mean, you don't understand Arabic?' the teacher said to me in Pashto. 'Are you a good Muslim?'

'Yes,' I answered, nodding my head.

'You're Khan, aren't you? I've heard … things … about you. Things I cannot repeat in front of a class of good Muslim boys. You are a dirty pig. Do you know that?'

I stared at my Qur'an, hoping for inspiration. The best course of action was to agree. I nodded my head, and laughter broke out along my bench, which was quickly silenced by the sound of the teacher's stick thwacking on his desk.

Two flies hovered over my head, breaking the hush that had fallen across the classroom. Instinctively I knew all eyes were on me.

'Mr Khan is going to read to us,' said the teacher slowly. 'Let's see how well he knows his Qur'an, boys. Ready, Khan? Begin.'

I felt like a runner on the starting blocks. The teacher jabbed his finger at a page, but I was so nervous I didn't notice which it was. To be honest, it wouldn't have made any difference if he'd pointed at the beginning, middle or end of the book. I couldn't read any of it, and the only bit that had ever stuck in my mind was the 'Al-Fatiha' – the opening seven verses. I took a breath and began.

Bismillāhi r-rahmāni r-rahīm
Al hamdu lillāhi rabbi l-'ālamīn
Ar rahmāni r-rahīm
Māliki yawmi d-dīn
Iyyāka na'budu wa iyyāka nasta'īn
Ihdinā s-sirāt al-mustaqīm
Sirāt al-ladīna an'amta 'alayhim ġayril maġdūbi 'alayhim
  walād dāllīn

(In the name of God, the Compassionate, the Merciful,
Praise be to God, the Lord of the Worlds,
The Compassionate, the Merciful,
Master of the Day of Judgement.
You alone do we worship, and you alone do we ask for
  help.
Guide us to the straight path,
The path of those whom you have blessed, not those
  who have deserved wrath, nor the misguided.)

As I spoke, I could hear the sounds of sniggering all around me. I ploughed on regardless, hoping the teacher would be impressed enough by this feat of memory to turn his focus away from me.

I finished and placed the Qur'an on the wooden rest in front of me. The sniggering had turned into open laughter, but instead of shouting for order, the teacher let the class carry on with the hilarity for a few moments, just to make sure my humiliation was total.

Finally he told them all to shut up. Then he turned his piercing gaze on me.

'So … the English boy has been wasting his time doing other things than studying his Qur'an,' he said, dragging out his words. 'A child of five could have recited those words, Khan. What did you think you were doing?'

'I … dunno. Was it wrong?'

The class members who understood Pashto exploded in laughter again. A lad in front turned round, pushing his tongue into his bottom lip and making the finger-twisting-temple gesture that means 'mental' in almost every country in the world.

'Not only were you wrong, Khan,' said the teacher, clearly enjoying my discomfort, 'you have shown deep disrespect to Allah. Now please find the right page and read what's on it.'

The boy next to me took my Qur'an and thumbed through it to the correct page. Then he passed it to me and sat back, waiting for the fun to begin all over again.

I stared at the page and its alien squiggles, and hot tears began to prick against my eyes. I closed the Qur'an and put it on my lap, bending my head at the humiliation of crying so publicly. The air was expectant with the horror of the terrible beating that would inevitably take place in just a few moments.

Without making a sound, the teacher stood up and made his way slowly to my row. When he reached the end, he stretched out his hand, beckoning me forward. I went towards him and he walked me up to the front and sat me in the teacher's chair, making me face the class.

'Perhaps you would like to give the lesson today, Khan?' he said. 'Tell the class all about life in England and how Muslim boys like you are diverted from the true path. Because that's what's happened, hasn't it?'

Before I could answer, he grabbed my hair and yanked me onto the floor, shoving me to my knees. He looked old, but he was incredibly strong. He pushed my face so far to the floor that I thought my nose was going to burst. Then he pulled my head up again so that everyone could see what a disgraceful waste of space I really was.

'Sit up straight and cross your legs, Khan!' he ordered.

I did as I was told. The teacher stood directly behind me so that I couldn't see him. Then he walloped me so hard with his stick on either side of my neck that it felt as if he was trying to chop off my head.

Instinctively I put my hands up to protect myself from any more blows and he expertly caught my fingertips with the stick's sharp edge. Doubled over in pain, I could barely breathe. The wind was literally beaten out of me. Even Rafiq's rage-fuelled excesses were nothing on this. The teacher was truly an expert in the art of punishment. And there was more to come.

With the end of his stick he forced me to sit upright in the cross-legged position. Then he stood by my side and hit me very hard indeed along the insides of my thighs. The pain was excruciating and when he stopped and ordered me to stand up I found that I couldn't. Two of the prefects who'd been watching the action unfold came to the front and, grabbing an arm each, hauled me back to the bench.

'Right,' said the teacher, 'let's carry on where we left off.' He pointed to a boy. 'You, read the passage I indicated. Khan will be listening very carefully, because he will be reading it for us tomorrow morning. Do you understand me, Khan?'

It was as much as I could do to nod my head.

I spent the rest of the lesson with my head down, not daring to look up in case I caught the teacher's eye and the whole horrible humiliation began again. I couldn't believe school was like this. I'd seen English kids coming home from the local primary, swinging their bags around and laughing. Had this been happening to them too? They'd looked too happy to have had a teacher like this one. I didn't remember anyone like him when I'd been at primary school myself. And I didn't remember anyone pissing themselves with fear in the classroom, as I had just done. We knelt in prayer, and with discreet wriggling motions I made sure most of it was mopped up by my baggy *salwar kameez* trousers. I couldn't bear another thrashing – and I still had tomorrow to face.

Chapter Eleven

I lay awake most of that night, pain and worry keeping me from any chance of a decent sleep. But the following day came and went without incident, and so did the day after that. I wasn't asked to read or recite. In fact the teacher never as much as looked at me during the lessons. Neither did anyone take any notice of me in the mosque. The prefects marched up and down on the hunt for boys who weren't praying properly, but while it was obvious I was copying my neighbours, I wasn't picked up on it.

Even so, there was no one I could ask to help me with the Qur'an. Also, there seemed to be no physical way out of the place. The thought of leaving, by any means possible, was on my mind constantly. There was no point asking permission from the imam. This wasn't some kind of public school where you could just pop home for the weekend. It was clear that running away was the only option. But even if I did escape I had no idea where to go; from what I'd seen on the way here, the landscape outside was brutal desert. I was resigned to my fate. Eventually I might learn the Qur'an and become one of those older boys, growing a bushy beard and whipping younger lads into line. Either that, or I would simply be beaten to death. I could easily imagine it happening. After all, who was there to protect me? Who cared anyway?

When the beating didn't arrive I wondered whether the teacher was deliberately ignoring me and just getting on with educating those who might become teachers or imams. So it was with far less apprehension that I entered the classroom on my fourth day at Haqqania. I picked a seat towards the back of the classroom. I was confident that I wouldn't be called upon to read, but I didn't want to take too many chances and this seemed one of the safest places.

The door opened and the teacher strode in, the morning sun catching the henna highlights in his beard. He never looked anything less than furious, but at least he wasn't furious with me. As he walked to his seat I picked up my Qur'an and opened it at a random page, pretending that I knew what it said. I wasn't fooling anyone, least of all myself, but it seemed sensible to look as though I was trying.

The teacher opened his copy of the Holy Book and indicated the verse he wanted to begin with. There was general shuffling as the class found the correct page. With no chance of reading the Arabic page numbers, I stared fixedly at the page I was on.

'Now then, boys,' the teacher said, 'you will remember the incident a few days ago in which a student had no idea of what was said in the Qur'an.'

I carried on looking at my book. I knew he couldn't be referring to me. In the last couple of days there had been several beatings of boys who'd stumbled over their verses.

'Today I have decided to test that student again,' the teacher continued. 'I have very kindly given him three days to work on the verse and today he will be word perfect. Won't you, Khan?'

I didn't look up. I simply didn't think he was talking to me.

A hush descended on the classroom and a near neighbour nudged me in the ribs. The teacher was staring straight at me. He hadn't forgotten at all. He was just stringing this out so that when the time came, the lesson I would learn would be an exceptionally severe one.

My near neighbour turned the page of my book. It was the lad who'd greeted me on my first night at Haqqania, telling me where I was and that I must have been 'very naughty' to have been transported there by my relatives.

'Just try your best,' he whispered in bad Pashto, 'otherwise he's gonna kill you!'

'Can you help me?' I pleaded. 'I haven't a clue about this.'

'Mr Abdullaev! Face the front and shut your mouth!'

The lad immediately did as he was told, rolling his eyes at me to indicate that I was on my own.

'Now, Khan. Read.'

Of course I couldn't do it. I had no clue about this verse or any other verse in the Qur'an apart from those I knew by memory, and they were few and far between.

'Somewhere in England,' I thought, 'my mum is cooking bacon and eggs and going down the supermarket or watching telly or going on holiday – doing all the normal things that white people in England do.' I was her son, as much a part of her and her heritage as I was of my dad and his, and yet here I was in a situation unimaginable by any Western standards. I felt I'd been transported back a hundred or even a thousand years to a time when there were no cars, no music, no videos – nothing apart from religion and the endless burning sun.

'I can't,' I said finally. 'I just can't do it. I'm sorry.'

There was a pause as the teacher weighed up what I'd said. I'd basically admitted defeat. No doubt he would come down on me like a ton of bricks. I hunched forward, expecting a rain of blows from the prefects as they dragged me up to the front. But nothing came.

Finally, the teacher spoke. 'It appears Mr Khan needs extra tuition,' he said, without a hint of anger in his voice. 'You will stay behind after and we will work on the very basics. Yes?'

'Yes, sir,' I said. I could hardly believe it. Not only was I not going to get a beating, he was actually offering to help me. I turned to my neighbour and smiled. He didn't smile back.

'Come and see me afterwards,' he whispered.

I wanted to ask him what he meant, but someone had begun to read and I was intimidated into silence by the hovering presence of the prefects, who were always keen to lash out with their sticks. The reading dragged on until prayers and lunchtime, then it was back for another few hours of work that went completely over my head.

Class was finally dismissed just before evening prayers. I was instructed to return after I had prayed with everyone else.

'... and make sure you ask Allah, blessèd be His name, for extra support and guidance this evening,' the teacher added.

I nodded.

As usual we filed into the mosque hall for worship and once it was over the rest of the boys headed to the kitchen. I went back to the classroom, pleased to be getting some extra instruction but also nervous about a one-to-one with a man who only three days ago had beaten me savagely in front of the whole class.

'Now, Mohammed,' he said in a kindly voice as I opened the door, 'tonight's lesson will be very easy and will be held in another part of the building. Follow me.'

I did as I was told and followed him across the courtyard, beyond the kitchens and towards a cloister in a corner of the madrassa that I hadn't been to before. As we walked, I saw two men leading a mule laden with baskets of vegetables through the main gate. By the central well another pair of traders were smoking and drinking tea. Their mules were tied to a large iron ring cemented into the well wall. The men appeared to be in no rush. I guessed a madrassa containing a couple of hundred hungry boys was a guaranteed source of income to local people. But where was 'local'? I wondered where the nearest town might be and whether it was such a difficult journey that only a mule could make it safely.

The teacher opened a heavy wooden door and gestured to me to go into the room beyond. He flicked a light switch, but no sooner had the bare bulb come on than it went off again. I'd been here long enough to know that it was a power cut. The electricity supply in this area was patchy at best and already I was used to lights going off at random. The teacher said something, then shoved past me and lit two candles that were mounted on holders in the wall.

As the room came to life I could see there was a blackboard at one end of it and, fixed to the floor, a thick wooden beam with two loops of iron set about two feet apart.

With his stick, the teacher motioned me over to the wooden beam and made me stand on it. He bent down, grabbed my left ankle and pushed it into one of the iron loops, snapping the two halves together. Before I knew it he'd done the same with my right ankle. He'd imprisoned me in a leg brace, a device you might see in a museum of torture methods but not in July 1988, in a country that was in the United Nations and was meant to be civilized. I was 13 years old. And, young as I was, I knew there was something very wrong with what was unfolding.

'Now, Khan,' said the teacher, looking demonic in the flickering light of the candle, 'you have offended me and you have offended God even more. You are a very wicked boy and you must be punished. I will write a phrase in Arabic on the blackboard and you will repeat it and repeat it until you understand it fully.'

I could barely see the board and leaned forward to get a better look. The braces squeezed against my ankle bones and I reeled back in pain. As I did so, the tendons at the back of my feet were choked by the rough iron. I realized I couldn't sit or squat; I had to stand as still as a statue for however long the teacher was prepared to keep me in this position.

Carefully, he wrote the following words on the board in Arabic:

Bismillāhi r-raḥmāni r-raḥīm
Al ḥamdu lillāhi rabbi l-'ālamīn.

When he had finished, he indicated I should read them. I couldn't of course, and so he lashed me very hard several times across the backs of my legs with his stick. If I could have buckled I would have done, but the pain around my ankles was already intense and would only get worse if I flinched.

'You know this!' he screamed. 'You recited it in class! It's about the only damn thing you do know! Come on!'

Then I realized he was referring to the Al-Fatiha, the opening verses of the Qu'ran that had somehow stuck in my head. Was he giving me a way out? I recited the lines as slowly and clearly as I could, only to receive another series of blows across my legs and my shoulders. I cried out as the teacher slashed the stick backwards and forwards across my body.

'What kind of an accent is that?' he said. 'Again – and properly this time!'

I wanted to say that it was a properly flat Lancashire accent overlaid with a thick coating of Pathan, but that would've led me into more trouble. Instead, I tried again, and again, and got another dose of the stick.

It was clear this was going to go on and on. The teacher pointed at the words and pronounced them for me to follow. But every time I attempted it, it just seemed to make him more irate.

Finally, he'd had enough of me – but he decided to leave rather than let me go.

'I'll be back in two hours,' he said, 'and you'd better have learned it by then. Otherwise …'

With that he slammed the door shut and locked it from the outside.

So began two hours of what can only be described as torture. The leg braces hurt like hell. In the gloom of the cell there was nothing to focus on but the blackboard. I stood in silence for a minute, hardly believing this was happening. Then someone banged loudly on the door.

'Read those prayers out loud,' shouted a voice, 'or it will be worse for you!'

The voice wasn't that of the teacher. I guessed he'd posted a sentry – probably one of the prefects – outside the door to make sure I was doing what I was told. I began to recite out loud, my voice cracking with fear. At any moment the brutal bully could come barging through the door and give me a caning.

Over the next two hours I must've read those words about 4,000 times, each time trying to improve on the accent. The minutes dragged by agonizingly slowly and by the time a key was placed in the lock I was on the point of collapse. And I still sounded like a Pakistani Peter Kay.

The teacher entered and looked me up and down. 'I hope we're making a good Muslim of you, Khan,' he snarled. 'Now, read.'

I did, trying my best to sound like a native Arabic speaker. When I reached the end, the teacher lashed me three or four times across the back with his stick, then bent down to unlock my shackles. His long beard brushed against my bare feet and I shuddered. It felt as though spiders were crawling across my skin. Then he stood up and pushed me to the floor. I cowered in the corner, exhausted, as the bastard loomed over me.

'You're a disgrace to Islam, Khan,' he said. 'I was warned about you, but I didn't imagine you'd be so stupid. Go back to your room and pray to Allah, blessèd be His name, for forgiveness.'

He pointed his stick at the half-open door and I scuttled through it. Darkness had descended on the madrassa and the power was still off. I groped my way forward, the tears that I'd suppressed in the cell now flowing. I was glad no one could see me.

After wandering around in a circle for five minutes or so, I finally located the entrance to the dormitory. I pushed aside the hessian curtain across the doorway and, without looking at the prone bodies scattered all over the floor, made it to the corner where my grimy shawl lay. I crawled underneath it, screwing up my eyes to block out the horror of the last few hours.

'This isn't happening,' I told myself over and over again. 'I'm not here – it's all a dream. Tomorrow I'll wake up in England.'

But the grunting and farting of the sleeping boys all around me and the weird howls of wild dogs in the mountains above the madrassa told me different. I was here, and here to stay. This was a waking nightmare.

I lay curled up in the foetal position for some minutes, feeling very sorry for myself. Then I felt a hand shaking my shoulder. I shrunk further into the shawl, expecting a fist in my face. But the shaking was gentle.

'Hey, Khan – are you OK? It's Abad. Abad Abdullaev. From class …'

I looked up to see the face of the kid who'd sat next to me that day and had tried to help. At a guess he was about 16. The beginnings of a moustache were sprouting from his top lip. He had the same slightly Chinese look as the man who had admitted me.

'What happened? Let me guess – he locked you to the floor, huh?'

I nodded, not daring to speak in case I started crying again.

'Bastard. He did that to me when I first got here.'

Abad's Pashto was terrible, far worse than mine. But I could just about understand him.

'Is it true you're English?'

'Yeah. I should be there now. The family brought me here. I dunno why …'

'White girls is what I heard,' Abad said, grinning. Gossip travelled fast in this place. But it wasn't altogether true. 'White mum' would've been more accurate. But I didn't say that. It was too complicated to explain.

'I didn't do anything!' I said. 'We were only talking. If I hadn't got caught …'

'… you wouldn't be here. Bad luck, kid.'

From the far end of the dormitory someone shouted something in our direction. Abad replied in a language I'd never heard before and the voice fell silent. Abad wasn't tall, but he was wiry and tough-looking and had a feeling of 'don't mess' about him. By rights, he should be a prefect. I wondered why he wasn't.

'What's your first name?'

'Mohammed. People call me Moham.'

'OK,' Abad said, 'Moham it is. Listen kid, try to ignore that bastard teacher. He's trying to break you. If you start crying or anything, he'll keep doing it. I want you to sit next to me every lesson from now on, yeah?'

'Yes, OK. Will you help me?'

'I'll try,' Abad replied. 'I've been here long enough not to get beaten up anymore. But I'm not making any promises. And I'm not taking a battering for you. Understand?'

I understood – just. As slowly as I could, I told Abad that if he helped me with my Arabic, I would do the same with his Pashto. He shrugged as if to say 'Who cares?' but he agreed. We shook hands and he crept back to his bed.

My ankles were still red raw and painful. It had been one of the most awful days of my life. I pictured Haani and Sadeeq sitting in the doss-house back in Hawesmill, smoking fags and listening to Radio One, wondering how and when they could entice the next batch of giggling white girls in through the door. They had no idea of what could happen to them if their families decided they weren't behaving properly. Did they wonder where I was now? Did they care? Word had probably gone round that I was 'in Pakistan'. Nothing unusual about that. But I'd never heard of anyone stuck in the situation I was in now. Haani and Sadeeq didn't know how lucky they were.

But at least there was Abad. I wondered if I could trust him. I had thought I could trust Yasir, but how wrong had I been! Yasir had been nice to me right up to the point where he'd buggered off to the airport without a backwards glance. He must've known what was going to happen, the snake! I swore that if I ever saw him again, I'd bust his nose. The thought of seeing him go down, blood everywhere, cheered me up slightly.

Like Yasir, Abad was older than me, though only by a couple of years, and he seemed genuine. But how did I know he wasn't a spy for the teacher, or the imam or the mullahs who ran this place? If I trusted him and gave him enough information, they could really hurt me badly. I was very confused. I wanted to trust him, and more than anything I wanted him to help me, but I had to be careful. I decided to be his friend, but not to say too much about myself until I got to know him.

The next day I followed Abad around like a little lamb. He seemed pleased about it, as if he was my big brother. He was definitely respected around the madrassa. I watched how he walked into the classroom and the mosque, shoulders back, head held high, like a fighter going into the ring. No one was going to push him around. For the first time in years I had a protector. The only other person apart from Dad who'd been like this had been Qaisar, the cricket-loving holy man married to my cousin Ayesha. He'd been as kind as he could be, but his motivation was religion and getting on 'the right path'. I wondered if he knew I was here. No doubt he'd approve, but I was sure even he would've been horrified by the torture methods used on the students.

Even so, with Abad by my side I seemed to be getting off without any more beatings. For the rest of the week I sat next to him in class, listening carefully as he quietly pronounced the verses being read out and got me to whisper them back. The teacher and the prefects must've seen what was happening, but they left me alone for a few days. At the end of the week I was suddenly jumped on to read a verse and, with Abad prompting me under his breath, managed to get through to the end. There was the usual sniggering about my accent from the rest of the class, and at the end of the recitation I got a bit of the ear-pulling treatment and a stripe across my back from a prefect, but the teacher made no comment. Perhaps he thought I'd made an effort, if nothing else.

In what little spare time we had, Abad and I sat in a shady part of the courtyard and looked at the Qur'an over and over again. With 114 *suras*, or chapters, to choose from, it was pot luck whether we'd hit on one that was subsequently read out in class. But at least I was trying. In return I corrected Abad's Pashto and taught him new words. Anything I couldn't make him understand we worked out in sign language. Soon a kind of secret code emerged between us.

I also learned something about his past. He was from Uzbekistan and had been at Haqqania from the age of eight. His older brother had attended too. In eight years he'd never gone home once. He was now 16 and had seen 'many things' at the madrassa.

'There are some good people here,' he said, 'religious people who mean well. But there are some very bad people too. Not just our teacher. You understand?'

I shook my head. I'd no idea what he was talking about.

'One day, kid, I'll tell you,' he said. 'It's not safe for you to know right now.'

I thought he was being dramatic, in the way only wised-up 16-year-olds can be. But I took him seriously, too. If a mere teacher could get away with torture, what were the top people up to? At that moment I couldn't begin to guess.

Abad told me bits about life beyond the madrassa walls. There was a village nearby, he said, that senior boys, including himself, were allowed to visit once a week. This wasn't a day out; the boys were sent to collect spare food from the local people. The villagers were told it was a step on the path to heaven, and they gave willingly. I'd seen boys returning through the gate with large rice sacks full of things, but hadn't dared to ask what it was all about. Now I knew – and I realized the madrassa wasn't in such an isolated spot as I'd thought.

The days turned into weeks. After a while I fell into the routine of madrassa life, which was little more than pray, eat, read the Qur'an, eat, pray and sleep. I still felt lonely, afraid and more than a little stupid, particularly in lessons, but while I was still beaten, it was less frequently.

Under Abad's guidance I even learned the proper way to pray in the mosque. I copied him faithfully, listening for the cues to kneel, stand up, place the hands on the stomach, bend forward and stand up again, depending on the prayers that were being said and the time of day we were hearing them. I was (and still am) confused by the precise timing and was always half a second too slow, but Abad didn't mind me copying him. No one really noticed that I was out of time every time.

Chapter Twelve

I pestered Abad several times to tell me what he meant by the 'bad people' who had a connection with the madrassa. Although he shared bits and pieces of information with me, this was the one area that I couldn't get him to talk about. Soon I realized that when he said it wasn't safe for me to know, he wasn't exaggerating, and I finally gave up asking.

Friday was always a busy day at the madrassa. Across the Islamic world the *Jumu'ah*, or Friday prayers, is the most important gathering of the Islamic week. Attendance at mosque is compulsory and there are two sermons, one much longer than the other. It is said that anyone who goes to Friday prayers and remains quiet during the sermon has his sins between that Friday and the previous one forgiven. As students of the Qur'an, we had to carry out our devotional duties to the letter on that day.

However, there was also a lighter atmosphere on Fridays too. Traders selling hot food and fruit gathered outside the madrassa walls and after prayers older boys were allowed out to make purchases on our behalf. These little treats weren't much, but they made the end of the week slightly more pleasurable and I looked forward to them. It was also good to see the madrassa gates open for a change; the outside world didn't seem so remote when people were coming in and out.

One Friday, as we were eating lightly-cooked unpopped corn seeds in our usual shady corner of the courtyard, Abad nudged me in the ribs.

'Not now,' he muttered, 'but in a few seconds have a look over at the well. Don't stare – and don't catch anyone's eye.'

I carried on eating my popcorn seeds for a minute, then glanced casually towards the well. Around it was a group of men dressed in black *dishdasha* robes, heavily bearded and carrying AK47s. Some wore the round Afghan hats shaped like a pancake. They seemed relaxed, smoking and chatting with a handful of the madrassa's top people, including the Chinese man. They looked exactly like the men I'd seen in the roadside café on the way to Grandma's relatives in Afghanistan. Parked close by was a dusty brown open-backed pick-up truck piled high with wooden crates.

I finished my seeds, not wishing to attract attention. '*Mujahideen?*'

'Got it in one,' Abad replied. 'We're right in the middle of the fighting season. They've come here to rest for a while.'

'But why here?'

'Because most of them are ex-students. You know what *jihad* is, don't you?'

I shook my head. I'd heard the term but had no idea what it meant. When Abad explained, I realized that was what some people had been talking about around Hawesmill – how the brave Islamic fighters had stood up to the Russians in Afghanistan.

'The thing is, Moham, those guys are brainwashed by this place. They get told all sorts of stuff as kids and then they go out to fight and die for Islam,' Abad said.

'What's wrong with that?'

'Nothing's wrong with it,' he replied, 'if that's what you believe in. But is it worth dying for? Here, they'll tell you that it is.'

Abad told me that the older boys, including himself, often stayed behind after mosque for extra sermons. These explained the concept of *jihad* and how important it was to establish Islam as the main religion in every country of the world. The only way to do this, they were told, was to join the *mujahideen* and fight.

'We get told the West will resist,' he said, 'but we have to be strong, 'cos Allah will lead us to victory. These guys,' he indicated the men round the well, 'are like the shock troops. They're gonna pass on their knowledge to us – kids like me and you. That's what we're here for, to be honest.'

I was astonished, and scared too. Learning the Qur'an was one thing, dying for Islam another altogether. It had never struck me that people would die for their religion. I had thought the *mujahideen* were just trying to get the Soviets out of Afghanistan. I hadn't known there was another side to it – and I had never expected to be part of that war machine.

'That's why I didn't tell you, kid,' Abad said. 'Not right away. I didn't want you doing something stupid. Now you know.'

I asked him why he was still there.

'Nowhere else to go,' he said. 'For the moment, I just do what they say. But when the time comes, I'll be gone. One thing's for sure – I won't be dying for those people.'

He nodded towards the fighters, who had now stacked their weapons in a triangle and were sitting in a circle and sharing a bowl of curry, mopping it up with chapatis.

'You see in that truck? All those boxes? Full of AKs and ammunition. Rocket launchers, too, and grenades. This place is a weapons dump. Bet you didn't know that, either?'

Seeing the fighters and their weaponry and knowing what might lie ahead for me was more than I could take. It wasn't that I was unused to guns; people carried them in Tajak to protect themselves against bandits, and a house wouldn't be complete without an ancient-looking shotgun propped up in a corner. Hearing shots during the day and night was fairly common. People would fire at wild dogs trying to kill chickens, or simply shoot into the air in celebration of a wedding. It wasn't how things were done in the West, but neither was it anything military. But this was something different. These weapons were constant companions – cleaned, oiled and well looked-after. And, by the way the fighters casually slung them onto their shoulders, very well-used too.

I sat against the whitewashed wall and raised my face to the sun. The warmth felt good on my skin. I could smell fried food wafting from just beyond the gates, and all around the compound boys sat, ate, chatted, prayed and generally hung out. If you accepted what you were taught without question and with complete obedience, this was a good life. But I knew different. I knew how life was in other places and cultures. While not rejecting my own, I wanted to explore all those others. After all, I was as much a part of them I was of this. I knew that if my mum could see where I was, she wouldn't believe it. She would be angry that only one part of my heritage was being developed. She would be scared for me, too.

'I think I need to leave here,' I said.

'Like how?' Abad replied. 'There's you, running through the gate at top speed, and there's them, with their AKs. Who's going to win? Come on, Moham, grow up ...'

He was right. I hadn't heard of anyone who'd left this place simply because they wanted to. Would they kill a boy for trying to run away? I couldn't be sure, but I didn't want to take that chance. Abad was right – it was best just to sit it out until you were old enough and strong enough to exist out there without getting sucked into violence.

I stood up and dusted myself off.

'Going somewhere?' Abad laughed.

'Nowhere near them,' I said, nodding towards the black-beards by the well. 'I want to catch up on some study. See you at prayers.'

I wandered off towards the dormitories. I was 13 years old. It would be three years before I was Abad's age and ready to look after myself. I would be a senior boy then, maybe even a prefect. Would I be lashing out at little lads with a stick or hanging around the well with the *mujahideen*?

I didn't want to think about my future at Haqqania, but in the days that followed it was the only thing on my mind. The endless praying and reciting, the terrible food, the beatings and verbal abuse, the brainwashing – how much longer could I stand it? The thought that I was handing over my young life to the clerics was horrible. I started to cry myself to sleep most nights. Abad became worried about me. I was losing weight and occasionally nodding off in class. He warned me that to be caught sleeping while the Qur'an was being read would cause no end of trouble. I'd be sent back to the cell and the leg irons, possibly for a whole night. It had happened before, he said, resulting in broken ankles that never mended properly.

I knew Abad had my best interests at heart. He had asked me a lot about England and seemed genuinely interested in the West. He never made any nasty remarks about non-Muslims and he never flinched when I told him I had a white mum. He was a worldly guy stuck in a very unworldly place. Having weighed it up, I felt I could trust him with an idea.

Somehow I had to get back to England. I didn't know where we were, other than in the far north-west of Pakistan, and I'd neither money nor passport. OK, there were villages, but in between seemed to be desert. The odds were stacked against me, but I didn't care. I wanted to go home. Even I found it hard to believe, but I missed those rain-washed streets crammed with houses. I wanted to see Jasmine again and hang out with some of the local lads, if Rafiq would let me. I didn't even care about him; if he wound me up, I'd sit in my room and listen to the radio without him knowing. I wouldn't take any more shit from him, that was for sure. Then I reminded myself that he was the most likely reason for me ending up here. In that case, I would track down my mum, if she was still alive. I wasn't a little kid any more. I was 13, and I'd already been through a lot. What more could Rafiq do to hurt me? I vowed that when I got home I would run away and, whatever it took, find my mum. Dad's family would never put me through any crap again.

I waited another week, until the Friday, before unveiling my plan to Abad. I'd rehearsed it about a hundred times in my head to make sure Abad wouldn't laugh at me. Which was exactly what he did.

'Oh, kid, didn't you listen to what I said last week?' he said.

We were sitting in almost exactly the same spot, eating fried seeds and watching a fresh set of *mujahideen* hanging around the well.

'Those guys would shoot the legs from under you if you made a bolt for it on a Friday. You'd make great target practice. They're bored because they've got the Russians on the run. They don't care.'

'OK, so forget Friday,' I replied. 'How about Saturday? It's quiet. No one will see if I go out of the gate. Once I'm on the road I'll get a lift for sure.'

'Yeah, sure,' said Abad sarcastically, 'and where will you ask to be dropped off? London? Come on, Moham, you're not thinking straight.'

'I am! Don't take the piss, Abad. I want out. I don't care what happens once I get past the gate. At least I'll be free.'

'Free to get kidnapped,' said Abad. 'Free to get raped by some pervert, free to get drugged up by that lot,' he indicated the *mujahideen*, 'and sent out to fight. If that's your plan, kid, you're better off where you are, believe me.'

'OK, I'll go back to Tajak,' I said defiantly.

'Great idea. All the way back there, to be driven straight back here by Imran. Nice one.'

He was right, of course. I hadn't really thought beyond getting past the gate – if I made it that far. Even if the *mujahideen* weren't around, I had no idea if the imam or the teachers carried weapons. I hadn't seen any evidence of it, but I couldn't be sure. Lots of people carried them for protection. Why would religious men be any different?

Abad pulled on his thin little moustache as we sat in gloomy silence. He'd dampened my enthusiasm for escape. All I could see now was a future that looked very much like today and every other day I'd spent here.

Then, after a long pause, he spoke.

'Not the gate, kid. Over the wall.'

'Huh?'

'Over the wall. It's the only way.'

'But it must be 25 feet high! I'd break my neck.'

'You've never been out of here, have you? I have. So let me tell you something about this place.'

Abad told me the ground around the outside of the madrassa was very uneven. While the front walls looked very high on the approach, the back of the building was a different matter.

'When they built it, they chucked all the rubble and earth against the back wall,' Abad said. 'So in some parts it's only about 10 feet high.'

'Only?' I thought back to my attempted escape from the terrace house where the white girls hung out. That had been a drop of 15 feet – not much higher than the lowest point of the madrassa wall. I had been shit-scared then, but at least I hadn't been threatened with an AK47.

'It's either that or stay here,' Abad said. 'You've got a choice to make.'

'OK,' I said, 'I'll do it. It'll be OK. I'll make it. I know I will.'

Abad smiled. 'You've got more guts than you think, kid. Here's what we'll do …'

I settled back, excited, while Abad outlined a very detailed plan of action. Had he been thinking about this for a while? I wondered if he was something of a mind-reader. He was one of the most intuitive people I'd ever met. As I listened, I imagined him as a kind of army officer, planning a breakout from a prisoner-of-war camp.

First, we'd walk casually round the madrassa as many times as we could without being spotted, to see if we could find an access point to the top of the wall. Once we'd located that, we would work out how to get to the nearest village.

'There's a little bus station there,' Abad said. 'You can get a bus to Peshawar. Ever been there? No? OK, well it's a big place and no one's gonna track you down there. What did you say your village was called?'

I told him.

He nodded. 'Off the main road to Islamabad, right? I've been in that area. It's near the air force base, isn't it?'

'Yeah, almost right next to it!'

'Good. 'Cos no one in Peshawar will have ever heard of Tajak, but everyone knows the base. All you need to do is get a bus from Peshawar to there. Then walk to Tajak.'

'But you said Imran would drive me straight back …'

'Only if he catches you,' Abad said. 'I've given that some thought too …'

I listened wide-eyed to Abad's plan, wishing he could come with me. I asked him if he would, but he shook his head.

'I don't think so, kid. The family would suffer if I scarpered. I've got a little brother coming here next year. Imagine the trouble he'd be in because of me.'

'But won't you get in trouble if I escape?'

He smiled. 'Nothing to do with me, kid. Nothing to do with me.'

He pulled me up by the arm, thrusting his copy of the Qur'an into my hand.

'Come on, let's have a walk around the yard,' he said. 'You stick your nose in the Holy Book. Look religious. I'll give you a bit of instruction.'

Between lessons, we walked round the compound several times that afternoon. To anyone watching we would've looked like the dedicated young Qur'anic student and his older mentor. But if that same person had been listening, he'd have heard a very different story. As we strolled, Abad indicated the weak points along the madrassa's walls and the various options for getting over them.

'You've got one thing right, kid,' he muttered as he pointed to some incomprehensible verse in my Qur'an, 'Saturday is the day to go. Nice and early, just after prayers. You know how quiet it is then.'

It was true. After the frenzy of activity that was Friday, Saturday was usually calm. Even the imam and the teachers were more relaxed that day, and the prefects left their sticks by their beds. If I was going to do it, it would have to be then.

'I could go over tomorrow, Abad,' I said. 'What do you reckon? No point hanging about.'

'Wait a week,' he replied. 'I don't want to hold you back, kid, but some of those *mujahideen* guys will be staying overnight. If they spot you …'

His voice tailed off, but I knew what he was getting at. I couldn't stand another second of this place, but a seven-day wait was preferable to seven bullets in the back. If the *mujahideen* returned the following Friday, the plan would be scuppered again. All I had to do was wait, hope and pray that they didn't. And I did pray. At night, when no one was listening, I prayed to Allah to help me out of the madrassa and to some kind of safety. Looking back, it seems ironic that I was asking God to release me from His church, but I needed faith in something. I hadn't any experience of other religions or their gods. Allah would have to do.

That week, some of the brutality I'd been confronted with at the start of my time in the madrassa returned with a vengeance. I'd been there at least five months by then – although it's fair to say that I'd lost track of time – and while I'd made progress with my studies, it wasn't nearly fast enough for the teachers. I was caned several times in front of the whole class, with additional ear-pulling, arm-twisting and head-slapping. The usual snorts of laughter greeted every attempt I made at the Arabic. But now I let all the pain and humiliation wash over me. I could keep practising for months and years and one day I might be word perfect. But I didn't want that. I just wanted to go home to England. I didn't care what happened after that.

Perhaps I had a spark of defiance in my eyes, because after a couple of days' nastiness and torment the teacher left me alone for the rest of the week and I sat there, looking as devout as possible, while the days dragged on towards Saturday.

That final Friday night, after prayers and the evening meal, Abad slunk over to my space in the dormitory and squatted beside me.

'I've just had a quick scout around,' he said, 'and it's all clear.'

'What do you mean?'

'The fighters aren't staying. They've just left. There will be no one around tomorrow. You're off, kid.'

My heart leapt into my mouth and I immediately felt sick. After all these months, I was going. But how far would I get?

Suddenly the prospect of wandering through unknown territory, with the madrassa people possibly on my tail, didn't seem
as appealing as it had a few days previously. I had been full of
bravado then; now I was really scared.

Abad saw the look on my face. He gripped my shoulder and
squeezed it.

'Hey, don't worry,' he whispered. 'You'll be OK. I know it.'

'How?'

'Dunno. Just do. There's something about you, Moham.
You're a survivor. You'll get through.'

Tears welled up in me and I looked away. Abad was a true
friend, one of the very few people I'd met that I could trust. I
badly wanted him to come with me.

'What about you?' I said.

'Don't worry about me. I'm fine. Maybe I'll come to England
one day, eh?' He grinned. 'You can show me these white girls.'

I stifled a laugh, as I didn't want to wake anyone else up. I
also knew that I probably wouldn't see him again, and felt sad.
He'd saved my life here. How could I ever thank him for it?
And he still hadn't finished. From the sleeve of his *salwar
kameez* jacket he pulled two bits of paper. One was greenish in
colour and rolled up tightly in a cigar-shape. The other was a
map.

'It's rough, I know. But it's how I remember the road from
Peshawar to Kamra. Kind of. I've written in a few landmarks. If
you see those, you know you're on the right road. Good luck,
kid. Now get your head down and don't worry. I'll give you a
leg-up tomorrow.'

I shoved the bits of paper into my pocket, but before I'd had a chance to thank Abad, or tell him how much I'd miss him, he'd slipped off into the darkness.

I lay there for ages, thinking back to the day I'd arrived at Haqqania. I had been alone in the world, but there had been a safety net in the shape of Abad. Now I could only hope that that safety net would appear somewhere else, in another shape or form, and be just as effective. Nervous as I was, I pulled my old shawl over my head, blotting out any more memories of the madrassa and its crude, cruel methods of education. In no time I was asleep.

The muezzin's call to prayer woke me as usual and I stumbled out of bed. It only hit me as I walked towards the mosque, just one sleepy boy in a crowd of sleepy boys, that today was the day. My guts gave a lurch and instinctively I looked round for Abad. He was there, just to the left of me, but didn't acknowledge me at all. It was almost as though he'd never spoken to me in his life. What was he playing at? Was he detaching himself from me deliberately? Had he set me up for something? The thought of him being a madrassa spy or a traitor to our friendship filled me with horror. I'd been betrayed before by so-called friends. Could it happen again?

All through prayers I thought of nothing else. Abad was still keeping his distance. I tried to act as normally as possible, even though I was tearing up inside. I had the map and the other bit of paper Abad had given me inside my *salwar kameez*. I had my shawl, too, and my sandals. I was wearing all my worldly possessions. I glanced out of the mosque window. Two vultures were circling high above the minaret, lazily hovering and swooping before reaching for the skies once again. They seemed so carefree, and for a moment they gave me hope and inspiration. Then I pictured myself thirsty and tired, making my way across the desert with the birds of prey following me, waiting for the moment when I collapsed and couldn't go on. I shuddered and wished I wasn't doing this. But there was no alternative. I had to leave now, with or without Abad's help.

After prayers I deliberately lagged behind the other boys as they rushed to the kitchen for a breakfast bowl of cold curry.

I felt a tap on my shoulder.

'OK, kid?'

It was Abad, of course. He wasn't ignoring me, only waiting until the coast was clear.

'You ready?'

I nodded. Of course I was. I'd been waiting for this for what had seemed ages.

Casually Abad left the line for the kitchen and took a diversion to the left, opening his Qur'an as he went. As usual, I hurried to catch him up. He passed me the Holy Book and began talking, saying anything that popped into his head. Most of it was in his own language and I hadn't a clue what he was on about, so I replied in English. We looked as though we were deep in conversation and no one saw us slip round the back of some outbuildings and to the low point of the wall.

'So ... you know what you're doing, yeah? Over the wall, down the hill and into the village. Bus to Peshawar. Then look at the map, or ask. Simple, huh?'

'But how do I pay for the bus?'

Abad rolled his eyes in despair. 'The other bit of paper I gave you. You've still got it, haven't you?'

I fumbled in my pocket and brought out the rolled-up paper.

'Thank God for that,' he said. 'You've got 40 rupees there – four notes of 10 rupees. It's not much, but you'll get a couple of bus trips out of it and a bit of food. You'll have to scrounge or steal the rest. Don't lose it.'

He looked round.

'Right,' he said, 'let's do it.'

He shook my hand.

'See you around, Moham. Be good.'

I smiled. 'Ta ra, lad,' I said, in my best Lancashire accent.

'Ta ra, lad,' he replied, imitating me perfectly. 'Now get gone!'

With that, I put my foot into his clasped hands and he heaved me to the top of the wall. Even at full stretch I was still a couple of inches off, and for a second or so we swayed like a couple of film stars in a silent movie. Then Abad stood on tiptoes and I managed to get a hand round a jutting piece of stone. With all my strength, I heaved myself up to the top.

The view from up there was breathtaking, the morning mist clearing to reveal spectacular mountains and valleys. But this was no time for scenery. The drop over the other side looked sickeningly long. I lowered myself down until I was clinging on by my fingertips.

'Let go, Moham, let go!' Abad called from the other side.

I let go and a millisecond later landed on a rough pile of builders' rubble, twisting my ankle as I hit the ground. I swore loudly, gave it a quick rub, then half-hopped, half-ran down the hill, hardly able to catch my breath.

Stupidly and inappropriately, Tiffany's daft pop song, 'I Think We're Alone Now', was playing in my head, along with images of *mujahideen* fighters aiming their AKs at me. If I hadn't been so terrified, I'd have laughed. But at least I was free.

Chapter Thirteen

T he village of small mud houses that lay at the bottom of the hill wasn't far, but in my state of panic and fear it seemed miles away. As I stumbled, hopped and ran across the rocky ground, I stood on a dry twig that snapped in half with a crack. In any other circumstances the noise would've been insignificant, but now all I could imagine was that a *mujahideen* sniper was on my case, and my heart thudded in my ears.

After about 400 yards or so I slowed down. My ankle was killing me. I couldn't go on any further at that speed, so I began to walk as quickly as I could in the direction of the mud houses. Abad had sworn there was a bus station here. I'd pictured it as similar to the ones I'd seen in Preston and Blackburn – big places with lots of passengers milling around and red double-decker buses moving in and out. But this was Pakistan. Here a bus station was usually nothing more than a strip of cracked pavement and a few converted beaten-up vans giving no indication of where they were going.

Abad had stressed that I had to get on the right bus. 'For God's sake don't get on the one to Afghanistan,' he'd said. 'If you do, you'll never find your way back. And you'll end up in the *mujahideen*. Or dead. So be careful, kid.'

As I entered the village, looking warily right or left for any madrassa boys on the hunt for food, I spotted a handful of likely-looking vehicles: shabby, dusty and beginning to fill up with passengers, mainly women and children. I had no idea where any of them were going. The only option was to ask.

I approached the passengers and singled out a woman with three small children hanging off her. She looked tired and harassed and probably wouldn't take much notice of a teenager on his own.

'*Za Kamra la Zama*,' I said in Pashto. 'I'm going to Kamra.'

She looked at me curiously and my heart sank. It was stupid asking for directions to an air force base. It would arouse instant suspicion.

But then she nodded, saying the only word I wanted to hear: 'Peshawar.'

I pointed to the bus. 'Peshawar?'

She nodded again, waving her hand in the direction of the vehicle and pushing her children up the van step before her. I could've kissed her – which really would have aroused suspicion – but instead waited until she'd got on then followed her up the steps.

The van was already three-quarters full. I prayed that I didn't need to have bought a ticket beforehand. Luckily there was a conductor standing by the driver. He said something I didn't understand and held out his hand. I took the roll of green notes out of the pocket of my *salwar kameez* and handed them all to him.

'Peshawar! Peshawar!' I said the word several times to make sure he understood.

He undid the roll of notes. I hoped he wouldn't rip me off and take the lot. If he did, I'd have no option but to accept it and then come up with another way of getting to Kamra from Peshawar. But luckily the conductor took two of the green notes and gave me two back. At least I'd something left and wouldn't starve.

I squeezed in by a family with kids and grandparents in tow, thinking I wouldn't look so conspicuous among them. They weren't exactly delighted, but they budged up all the same and for the first time that day I began to feel slightly less than utterly terrified.

The bus waited by the road for five long minutes as the driver watched out for late-coming passengers. I desperately wanted him to put his foot down and get away from there. Over in the madrassa they might've already noticed I wasn't there. There wasn't a daily roll call, but I had the feeling the prefects knew who was around and who wasn't. I expected Abad to have concocted a story if anyone asked about me. However, that wouldn't last forever. Sooner or later they would come looking.

I sneaked a look at the madrassa, outlined against the sky with the morning sun turning its white walls an orangey-pink. It appeared to be all quiet up there. The gates were shut and no one was looking over the walls. Sometimes the muezzin would spend hours in the minaret, praying to God before making his routine announcements and calls to prayer. But he was old and I imagined his eyesight wasn't up to much. If he'd seen me at all, he'd probably mistaken me for a wild dog. Not so the *mujahideen*, but Abad had assured me they weren't there. I glanced behind me in case a mob of black-bearded men was walking towards the bus. There was no one there. I told myself to calm down. If I looked jittery, I would attract suspicion and might get turfed off the bus. I had to relax.

The driver started his engine and pulled away from the kerb. I watched as the village and the madrassa beyond it faded into the distance. I'd been warned against getting on the wrong bus, but right now I didn't care if I ended up in Timbuktu, just as long as I didn't have to go back to Haqqania.

As I settled back in my seat, my mind began to wander. Supposing I couldn't find safety in Tajak? In that case I would go to the airport in Islamabad and sneak on a plane. If that didn't work, I'd stop the first white man I saw in the street and ask him for help. And if he turned me away, I'd go to the coast and get on a boat. The mighty Indus river wasn't far from Tajak. If I followed it, I would end up at the sea. If, if, if … I was dog-tired and the sun was gaining in strength, heating the inside of the van like an oven. Before long my eyes closed and I felt my head dropping, then jerking upwards again. Within minutes I was asleep.

Between snoozes I woke up and stared out of the van window at some of the most beautiful countryside I'd ever seen. I'd missed most of this on the way to the madrassa. Now I was free to drink it in – the sun glistening off the tops of snow-capped mountains and rivers that snaked through fertile valleys, all shimmering deep blues and greens. There was plenty of desert, too, and I was very glad I hadn't tried to make the journey on foot. As I fell asleep again, the lushness of my surroundings mixed with bizarre dreams punctuated by every jolt and rattle from the rickety old van.

After an hour or so I woke up properly. The countryside had given way to a series of small villages, each one as shabby as the last. They all looked like Tajak, or the villages around it. The road felt smoother too. It could only mean one thing – that we were getting close to Peshawar.

In my mind's eye I'd expected the journey to take hours, if not days. Abad hadn't said how far Peshawar was from Haqqania and, given the surroundings of the madrassa, civilization had seemed to be on the other side of the world.

This final stretch of the journey was marked by a huge amount of banging and thumping from the roof of the van. The inside was full to bursting, so people were climbing on the roof for a lift. The van's speed didn't bother them in the slightest and as we neared the outskirts of the city more and more people clambered aboard.

The familiar routine of passengers gathering bags and organizing children started as the bus neared its final destination. I sat tight, wondering if we were in the right city. Then the conductor shouted the name of the destination. Within seconds, the inside of the bus was a jumble of bags, children, old people and youngsters like me all fighting to free themselves of the airless, cramped conditions. I scrambled out of the seat and was given a firm dig in the ribs by an elderly woman in a bright green sari. I'd been asleep on her shoulder for most of the journey. There was no way she was letting me off before her, and I stood back so she could pass me. She muttered a few words in my direction and bustled off.

I stepped down into chaos. I thought I was used to typical Pakistani pushing and shoving, but a few horns honking in the middle of Tajak had absolutely nothing on the welcome I received during those first few minutes in Peshawar. Cars, buses, vans and motorbikes fought for space in the teeming street while donkey carts and their owners ambled along, oblivious to the blaring horns and yelling drivers. People pushed and shoved their way along cracked uneven pavements lined with cheap cafés, food stores and vehicle repair garages. Fully-veiled women strode past, dragging handfuls of screaming, fighting, crying children. I was mesmerized by the sights and sounds, and wanted to put my hands over my ears and just curl up by the roadside. The long silences around the madrassa, interrupted only by the wail of the muezzin and occasional shouts from angry teachers, had spoiled me. Now the modern world was right in my face and I couldn't stand it.

Anxiously I looked around for a van that might take me to Kamra. The scruffy signs written on bits of cardboard and stuck in the windows of the waiting vans meant nothing to me. I asked a couple of passers-by, but they just stared at me as if I was mad and walked on.

I stood for a few moments wondering what to do. I couldn't stay in this chaos. Perhaps there was a shop I could ask at. I started across the road, carefully avoiding all the maniacs on four wheels, two wheels or four legs, and headed for a grocer's shop, its frontage piled high with colourful and mouth-watering fruit.

'If the owner doesn't know where Kamra is,' I thought, 'he won't notice if I borrow an orange on the way out.'

I was hungry and thirsty, not having eaten all day. But as I got to the other side of the road I felt a tug on my shirt that was hard enough to stop me in my tracks.

'Hey, you. Yeah, you! Where are you going then?'

A lad around my age but a good few inches taller was speaking to me in Pashto. I understood him perfectly, but didn't reply. Something about his look and the cocky way he was standing, keeping a tight grip on my shirt, was very unsettling. Beside him was another youth, about 12 years old, with a grimy face and T-shirt to match. The pair looked tough and street-wise. Instinctively I knew they'd been watching me. At the time I thought I blended in well; with my *salwar kameez* and pale skin, I was sure I didn't look any different from anyone else around there. With hindsight I see that I must've stuck out like a sore thumb; either that or I just looked bewildered and naïve.

The older lad transferred his grip to the top of my shirt, just below the neck.

'You got any money?' he muttered. 'Come on, you must have …'

I shook my head and said 'no' in my best Pashto accent. They looked at each other in shock, then the lad pulled me closer to him. I hadn't fooled anyone.

'Hey, you're English. Aren't you? You shouldn't be wandering around here, you know. Someone might steal your money.' He grinned, then dived into my *salwar kameez* pocket. 'Come on, rich boy – give it me now!'

I'd liked to have told him about why I was here – Rafiq and the white girls, Yasir and his betrayal, Imran and the kidnapping, then the escape from the madrassa. Maybe if I'd sat down with these two over a Coke they'd have understood. But they were robbing me, pure and simple, and I couldn't afford to lose a single rupee.

I twisted away, wrenching the older lad's hand out of my pocket and sending him spinning to the ground. The other boy threw a punch at me but missed. I shoved him out of the way and started running, bashing into a nearby stallholder who screamed and yelled at me. The older boy was up and on his feet by now and the pair tore after me through the crowded street. Several people tried to grab me as I ran, probably believing I was a shoplifter, but they couldn't keep a grip on me. Fear made me strong and I ran like hell. In the chase one of my *charpal* open-toed shoes came off. I'd no time to retrieve it and carried on running, ducking down side-streets and across patches of waste ground.

I ran into a graveyard and dodged behind a tall tombstone, squatting against the cool marble. I was completely exhausted.

When I got my breath back, I peered round the side of the stone. The graveyard was deserted, and there was no sign of my pursuers. I was very grateful for that, but deeply worried too. In my haste to get away from the street robbers I'd run blindly, not taking any notice of where I was going. It was now approaching early evening and the chances of success-fully finding my way back to the bus station and finding a vehicle to take me to Kamra were slim. Also, I didn't know how far Kamra was from Tajak. If I arrived there in the middle of the night, it would scupper Abad's plan. I could try to find my way back to the station now and sleep there until dawn. But supposing the young muggers were still around? I didn't want to take my chances as dusk approached. I would have to sleep somewhere in Peshawar and try my luck in the morning.

I didn't fancy lying down in the graveyard, so close to the dead. The place reminded me of standing by my dad's grave in Tajak and asking him why he'd abandoned us. The lengthening shadows across the tombstones gave the place a creepy atmos-phere. I wanted to leave.

After a final check to make sure the lads weren't about to ambush me, I walked out of the cemetery gate and into a shabby street. A few people were knocking about, but no one took any notice of me. With my missing shoe and dirty *salwar kameez* I looked like a street kid. I guessed there were plenty of those in Peshawar.

I wrapped my shawl tightly around me and wondered where I might find some shelter. I didn't fancy a shop doorway – too public. And I didn't want to hide down an alleyway where no one would hear me scream if I was attacked.

On the opposite side of the road was a truck. It was just off the main street, but not so far that it was hidden from view. One of its tyres was completely flat. It looked as though it hadn't moved in a long time. Its back doors were locked and bolted. I had no chance of climbing inside, but I figured that if I got underneath it I would be hidden from view. All I could do was pray that no one decided to change the wheel in the middle of the night and drive off.

The coast was clear. Quickly I slid under the truck and curled up against the front wheel. In the dusk, I looked like a bundle of rags. That was fine by me. From where I lay I could just about see the night sky and the millions of stars that had enchanted me so much when I'd slept outside in Tajak. I had a powerful, almost overwhelming feeling that my mum was watching over me, willing me to stay safe and complete my journey home.

Although I was in grave danger if the truck moved, I felt settled in my makeshift bed – certainly safer than I'd ever felt in the madrassa dormitory. Here I could make my own decisions. I've been lucky in that I've always slept well, whatever the circumstances, and it was the same that night. Even with vehicles going past, footsteps only inches from my head and the occasional stray dog sniffing me out, I was soon out for the count. It had been a hell of a long day.

* * *

Alexander Khan

I woke up at dawn, cold and very hungry. I'd slept deeply, but my back was stiff from the uneven road surface. At least I hadn't been squashed by a 10-ton truck. Already people were going about their business – to mosque, to their shops, workplaces and cafés. I would blend into the crowd, and certainly looked dirty and scruffy enough to be taken for a native street kid. My accent gave me away, but if I avoided opening my mouth I figured I'd be fine. I threw my shawl over my shoulder and walked in the direction I thought would lead me to the bus station.

Twenty minutes later I ended up back by the broken-down truck. I felt like crying but I didn't, not wanting to attract attention. I set off again, this time taking a completely different route. A couple of buildings looked familiar and I half-recognized a market stall piled high with watermelons that I'd dashed past, but other than that I could've been anywhere in Pakistan. I needed to ask someone.

There he was, standing on the street corner watching to see if anyone was looking at him. Like so many men in this city he was thin, wore *salwar kameez* and had a moustache. Unlike many others he was wearing an 'NYC' baseball cap and ludicrous outsize gold-coloured Nike trainers with fat laces. This was a man who'd been abroad and was desperate for everyone to know it. He was smiling broadly at those who smiled at him, no matter whether they were genuinely impressed or simply taking the piss. If he'd been abroad, I figured he'd know some English.

'Hey,' I said in Pashto, just in case I was mistaken, 'I like your trainers. Where did you get them?'

'London,' he replied, beaming. 'I've just been there, to see the family. Ever been?'

'Only to the airport,' I replied in English.

The guy looked at me in astonishment. 'You're English! Where from? What you doing here?' He looked round. 'Where are your parents?'

'I'm from Hawesmill,' I said, expecting he'd have no idea where that was. 'My dad's dead. I'm staying with relatives in Tajak. I need to get back to them. Do you know where the bus station is, please?'

The man laughed so hard his shoulders shook. 'Hawesmill! I can't believe it. I was there only three weeks ago, visiting my uncle. You might know him.'

He said a name, but I didn't recognize it and shook my head.

'I don't know him. I don't go out much. Only to mosque.'

I didn't want to get into a conversation about various people around Hawesmill. Sooner or later he would stumble across someone I knew – like Rafiq – and my face would give the game away.

'Good boy,' he said, patting my head. 'So, you're looking for the bus station. What brought you here in the first place?'

'I was on an errand,' I lied, 'and I got robbed. I ran away from them, but now I'm lost.'

'Walk with me,' he said. 'I'll show you where it is. Now let me tell you about London …'

Off we went, the man talking ten to the dozen about the Houses of Parliament, Buckingham Palace and McDonald's restaurants. These places were as alien to me as Peshawar, but I chatted along with him, throwing him questions now and then to make sure we didn't get onto the subject of Hawesmill.

'You look half-starved,' he said as we passed a samosa stall. 'Want one?'

He bought a handful of samosas and gave me a couple. I almost choked them down. He smiled and gave me another one, telling me to put it in my pocket for later.

We reached the bus station. The man had a quick scout around and pointed to a converted van.

'OK,' he said, 'that bus is going by Kamra. You know it? The air force base?'

Of course I knew it. It was just as Abad had said – 'Get to Peshawar and ask for Kamra. Anyone will tell you.' Not for the first time, I thanked God that I'd met him. I hoped he hadn't got into trouble and said a silent prayer that Allah would keep him safe.

The man gave some coins to the bus conductor and nodded at me. I thanked him and he flashed a big smile at me and adjusted the angle of his baseball cap. He liked to think he was a big shot and I'd no doubt he was showing off to the conductor by paying for me. But I couldn't fault his generosity.

'Good luck!' he shouted as I climbed aboard. 'Remember my uncle. If you see him, tell him Majeed Shah says hello!'

'I will,' I said, waving goodbye.

I wondered what was happening in Hawesmill that very minute. It seemed strange that an old Pakistani man was wandering those streets he could never call home while I was here in the city he'd left many years before for the chance of a better life. I looked out at the same scenes I'd witnessed yester-day. It seemed slightly less chaotic, but it was still morning and there was plenty of time for the madness to really crank up as the day wore on. Would Majeed Shah's old uncle be happier here than in Hawesmill? Having experienced both places, I wasn't sure which I'd choose, but I knew one thing: my heart was in England. Despite everything, it was home.

Twenty minutes later the bus started off with a jolt. I'd no idea how far Peshawar was from Kamra or what I would encounter when I finally got off. I hoped the man had told the conductor to give me a shout when the bus reached my stop. If not, I was sure I'd know where we were – as long as I didn't sleep through and miss it altogether. I settled back, determined not to nod off.

True to form, I was asleep within 15 minutes of the bus leav-ing the station.

Chapter Fourteen

The journey was long, two or three hours, and I slept through most of it. I was jerked awake when the bus made scheduled stops. At one point everyone got off to buy fruit from a street seller. Not wanting to spend any money, I stayed in my seat, trying not to think about the juicy fruit being brought on board and consumed greedily.

As the morning wore on, the landscape began to look familiar. Villages lay by fields four feet high with crops of corn and wheat. Along the side of the road farmers led pack animals laden with fruit and vegetables to market. And, of course, there were the mosques. No matter how poor the village, the mosque would always look pristine, its gleaming minaret pointing proudly into the sky.

I thought about Haqqania. Many families in villages like the ones we were passing would give their eye teeth to send a son to a madrassa. I'd just escaped from one and was returning to a deeply conservative and religious environment. However I dressed it up, leaving an educational establishment like

Haqqania would look like ungratefulness at best; at worst, an insult to Islam. Abad had said that the most dangerous part of my journey would begin when I stepped off the bus at Kamra. It was possible that the first person I encountered in Tajak would be Imran and he would take me straight back to Haqqania under lock and key. Then they would ensure I never escaped again. I had to be very, very careful.

I saw Kamra before the conductor shouted out its name, extra loudly so that I would hear. We passed the high corrugated steel walls topped with barbed wire and watchtowers and I knew we'd arrived. I grabbed my shawl and pushed my way to the front of the van. The conductor blocked the exit and held out his hand. I fished in my pocket and pulled out the two remaining 10-rupee notes, both of which he took. I didn't know if that was the real fare or not, but I was in no position to argue. I stepped off the bus and watched it disappear into the distance.

The road before me shimmered with the heat. I had about four miles to walk, but it wouldn't be along this road. I remembered Abad's words as he described the rest of the plan: 'Get off the road as soon as possible. If someone sees you, you've had it. Get into the fields straight away and move slowly.'

Abad had asked if there were any buildings close to the family's compound. I'd told him about an old barn that belonged to a nearby farm. Cattle occasionally wandered into it, but by and large it was empty.

'Perfect,' he'd said. 'You must make for this place, and try to get there before noon.'

I looked up at the sun. It was almost at its highest point. Despite Abad's advice, I had to move quickly. Time wasn't on my side and I needed to get to that barn. A wrong move here and I could be back in Haqqania before sundown.

I peeled off the road and, following my nose, walked into a field full of watermelons. As Abad had suggested, I skirted round the outside of the field, taking advantage of gaps in walls and hedges to slip into the fields beyond. I was still hopping along on one shoe, trying to avoid the deep man-made pools of water used to irrigate the bone-dry earth. I kept a lookout for snakes and wild dogs; snakes could rear up suddenly if disturbed, so I was careful where I put my feet. Dogs were a bigger danger. I was used to seeing them around Tajak, eating from rubbish heaps and roaming around in large packs. Occasionally there would be a cull of them, and rightly so; they were full of disease and if you got bitten there was every chance you'd contract rabies.

I slipped behind trees and watched carefully as local farmers, silhouetted against the flat landscape, began to down tools and walk towards their homes. The hottest part of the day was almost upon us; I had to get to that barn very soon.

After two or three more fields I came to the outskirts of the village. There in the distance was the compound and about 200 yards in front of it the barn I was heading for. I stood still for a moment, unable to believe that only yesterday I'd scaled over a high wall some 200 miles from here and made it all the way back – a bit dirty, scuffed up and minus a shoe, but unscathed. In my head I heard Abad's warning once again: 'That will be the easy part, kid. After that – watch out.'

I slipped into the barn and lay flat on my belly. The midday sun had made the walk exhausting and I was desperately thirsty. But I couldn't think about that now. My focus was on the compound and anyone going in or out of it. Abad had told me what I already knew: that the hottest part of the day was when everyone found some shade and rested for a while. Farmers lay under trees, shopkeepers snoozed beneath canopies, housewives left their cooking and cleaning and stretched out on their beds. It was a normal part of everyday life and everyone stuck to it. Walking around in the midday heat was a sure sign of madness, local people said. So, according to Abad, this was the best time to get into the compound without Imran seeing me. Wherever he was, he would be snoozing. If I could slip past him and make it to Aunty Alia's room I would have a much better chance of being protected from his rage when he found out I'd returned.

'But she didn't do much the first time round,' I'd protested. 'She didn't stop Imran from taking me – no one did. Why would she be different this time?'

'There's no guarantee,' Abad had told me. 'But the fact that you've made it all the way back to Tajak must say something. From what you tell me, she's got power in that family. It's worth taking the chance, kid. What other options have you got?'

The answer was none. If Alia couldn't protect me, I was done for. But what Abad had said was true: she might have been a housewife, but she was a strong character and I'd seen her stand up to the men when necessary. She was respected for that.

The sun was at its peak. I slipped from my hiding place, my heart pounding, and picked my way carefully across the two fields in front of the compound. I hoped to God I wouldn't stumble, literally, over the sleeping Imran. Luckily, the field was empty of people and the only look I got was from a curious cow tied to a tree in the far corner.

My plan was to avoid the main gate and go in through the side entrance. Only the immediate family used it and while there was still every chance of encountering Imran, it was far less risky than being spotted by one of his cronies who happened to be walking past the front gate.

I reached the corner of the building and flattened myself against it army-style, looking left and right for trouble. The coast was clear.

I slid along the wall to the rusty iron gate. It was almost always unlocked; I hoped today would be no exception. I took a sidewards glance through it. There appeared to be no one in the immediate vicinity. Time seemed to stand still as I reached over to the latch and lifted it, then gently pushed the gate. It opened with a long creak and I winced, putting my hand up to my eyes. When I took it away, the gate had swung right back. It was now or never.

I crept in and flattened myself against the wall. There was no one around. The day beds under the canopy of vines, where I'd slept so contentedly at night, were unoccupied. A slight breeze ruffling the leaves of the orange tree was the only disturbance in the sleepy courtyard.

Then, a flash and the sound of footsteps. I squeezed myself up against the mud wall, hardly daring to breathe, and looked in the direction of the movement. There it was again, a glimmer of gold and red against the green of the eucalyptus bushes. I craned my neck as far as I dared. About 20 yards away was a child, maybe eight years old, playing in the dirt. It was Parveen, the daughter of Uncle Hussein who had been my partner at the odd little party held in the compound a week or so after my arrival. I'd still not figured out what that was all about, but at least she knew I wasn't a stranger.

'Parveen!' I whispered as loudly as I could. 'Parveen! Come over here!'

The child looked up, startled, her head darting backwards and forwards as she tried to locate the source of the sound. I knew that if she screamed she could give me away.

'Parveen!' I whispered, this time more softly. 'Over here, by the wall. It's Moham … your cousin.'

Cautiously, Parveen came towards me. I stepped out from the shadows and she saw me and smiled. 'Hi, Moham,' she said. 'Why are you hiding? Do you want to play a game?'

My few months away had obviously made no impact on her whatsoever. People come and go out of children's lives and they're largely forgotten. Parveen was talking to me as if I'd never been away.

'Yeah, I will play, but, ummm, not just yet. Is Aunty Alia around?'

Parveen pointed at Alia's house. 'In there. Asleep. Shush, don't wake her up, she'll be cross.'

'OK,' I whispered, going along with the game. 'I'll just go and say hello – be back in a minute. But don't tell anyone you've seen me. It's a surprise.'

Alexander Khan

I put my fingers to my lips and Parveen understood. She scuttled back to where she had been playing.

I breathed a sigh of relief. All I had to do now was get across the courtyard and into Alia's house without anyone else seeing me. Boldness seemed the best policy, so I strolled across the yard as though it was the most normal thing in the world and straight in through Alia's front door. She would be upstairs in the sleeping quarters. I pulled back the hessian cloth across her bedroom door and there she was, completely out for the count.

I hesitated for a moment. Then I sat gently on the edge of the bed and touched her bare foot as lightly as I could. I didn't want to startle her.

'Aunty … Aunty Alia. It's me, Mohammed. Wake up. I want to talk to you. You have to wake up.'

I had visions of Imran bursting in any second and catching me before I had chance to speak to her. I shook her foot harder and finally her eyes opened, at first sleepily and then wide in shock.

'Mohammed! Oh my God! Is this a dream? How did you get here? I thought you were … away.'

'It is me. You're not dreaming. I got out. Escaped from those evil bastards. They thought they could keep me there forever. No way. You know who I'm talking about, don't you? You know where I've been.'

Alia looked away in shame. 'Oh, Mohammed, I'm so sorry,' she said. 'If I could have stopped them, I would have. I tried, but they wouldn't listen. They said it would be good for you. I didn't know what to think. Maybe it would've been, I don't know …'

Her voice tailed off. She could barely look at me and I could sense how ashamed she felt.

'It's OK,' I said, taking her hand, 'I'm not angry. Not at you. But they kidnapped me. You know that. They took me away and I didn't want to go. They treated me like shit at that place!'

I couldn't believe I'd sworn in front of her, but I was starting to get mad. If Imran had walked in at that moment I'd have gone for him.

'I'm sorry,' she repeated, starting to cry. 'I couldn't do anything to stop them. I've stuck up for you, Moham, but this time it didn't work. Please believe me.'

I didn't like seeing her upset, so I calmed down. This was the moment I'd been waiting for.

'I need your help,' I said. 'I don't want Imran to catch me. Can you make that happen? Please, Aunty! I just want to go home to England.'

She paused, then said, 'It will be fine. I'll speak to Grandma. She'll know what to do. She ... doesn't know that you went to Haqqania. She thought you went home. She will be shocked and upset. But she will do the right thing, I promise you.'

Alia suddenly looked tired.

'I've been so worried about you,' she added. 'I knew you'd hate it there. What did they do to you?'

I didn't want to cry, not at that moment, so I shook my head. That told her all she needed to know and she sat up and hugged me. It was rare for a Pakistani woman to hug a male, even a relative, over the age of about eight, but she was obviously overcome.

'Don't worry,' she whispered, 'you're safe now.'

'What about Imran?'

Alia bit her lip. 'It's good news and bad news. The good news is that he's got a job in Dubai. Some kind of construction project. Lots of village men are working on it.'

'What's the bad news?'

'He doesn't go for another two days. He's trouble, Mohammed, and if he catches you he'll send you straight back. You'll have to hide in my house until he's gone.'

'I've made it this far,' I said. 'He isn't gonna catch me now. I can keep quiet for a couple of days. Oh – Parveen's seen me. Will she tell?'

'She's only a child,' said Aunty Alia, 'she'll be doing something else now. Don't worry about her. If she tells her father I'll say she was out in the sun too long. Now it's time you weren't here. Go into the other bedroom and keep the door shut. I'll go straight round to Grandma's and tell her. Then if he catches you, there are two people on your side and I wouldn't like to see Imran face down Grandma.'

She stood up and brushed herself down.

'Have you had anything to eat or drink?'

'I've had next to nothing for two days,' I said. 'I'm starving.'

'Good,' she replied, 'because I've got some fresh lemon sherbet and last night's curry. Will that do?'

I laughed, for what felt like the first time in weeks. 'Thanks, Aunty. Sounds delicious. Don't worry, I won't make a sound.'

'Into the next room then,' she said, 'and just keep your head down. You can manage that for two days, I'm sure. When

Imran's gone back to work you can tell me all about your adventures. You're quite a boy, aren't you? I think you'll go far.'

'Only as far as England,' I said as she closed the door.

A short while after, Alia returned with the lemon sherbet and curry, which I wolfed in seconds. She told me that Imran was due home in an hour or so and that I should be ready to stay in the room and be as quiet as possible.

'You shouldn't get too much trouble from him,' she added. 'He's packing for Dubai and he's very distracted by that.'

'You don't think anyone from Haqqania will contact him, do you?'

I'd been fretting about this ever since I'd made it over the wall. The family didn't have a phone, but it wouldn't be difficult for Haqqania's imam to contact his counterpart in Tajak's mosque. If that happened, the news of my escape would be broadcast from the minaret, and Imran wouldn't fail to hear that.

Alia paused for a moment and bit her lip.

'I don't know,' she said, running her fingers through her hair. 'I really don't know. It could happen. Word spreads like wildfire in places like this. I won't lie – if he finds out, he will come to hunt you down. You'll have to clear out – sleep in the fields or somewhere. It will be safer for you.'

'And you too.'

'Yes,' she said. She looked drawn and nervous. What Imran would do if he found she'd been harbouring me was no one's business. And if he found me, well …

I was terrified of leaving the shelter of Alia's house. I didn't want to come this far only to be discovered asleep under a tree.

The religious farmers around here would take a certain pride in finding a runaway madrassa boy and returning him to his teachers. They would see it as carrying out God's work.

'Don't worry,' Alia said, noticing my discomfort and pushing her own fears away, 'I'm sure it won't come to that. In fact, I'm going to speak to Grandma.'

With that, she left, shutting and locking the door behind her. I trusted her to stand up to Imran. The question was; was she strong enough? He would only need to persuade my uncles Hussein and Ajmal that it was in everyone's best interest that I go back and it would be a done deal. If he contacted Rafiq, who I was sure was behind all this in the first place, that would strengthen his argument all the more.

I curled up tight in the bed, trying not to let my imagination wander too far. Again I came back to the thoughts that constantly haunted me: why did Mum go away? Why did Dad die and leave us in the care of Rafiq? Why was I tricked into coming to Pakistan in the first place? So many questions and so few answers. Trapped in that small, stiflingly hot room, waiting for a knock on the door that would see me back in the madrassa, I swore that one day I would find out the truth, even if it took me the rest of my life. I didn't want revenge – although I sometimes had dreams of doing dreadful things to Rafiq – I just wanted the truth.

I lay there for hours, just staring out of the mesh-covered window at the sun as it headed west, bringing evening with it. I wondered what Alia had said to Grandma and whether Imran was on the prowl outside.

Presently someone opened the door. It was Alia.

'I've spoken to Grandma,' she said, 'and she wants to see you now. She's devastated and angry that no one told her where you'd gone. She says she's been betrayed. I've had to persuade her not to go and see Imran and give him a piece of her mind.'

'But what if he sees me going round?'

'He won't. He's been and gone. He's over at the *baytuk*, saying goodbye to his friends. He'll not be back for ages.'

So Imran was at the café he'd taken me to after he'd forced me back into the van at Islamabad airport. No doubt the men he'd enlisted to tie me up and transport me to Haqqania would be there with him, drinking tea, smoking and laughing. The bastards.

'He's off to Dubai in the morning,' Alia added, 'a day early. Come on, Mohammed, don't be afraid. It's good news – only a little bit longer to go.'

I knew from bitter experience that life could change rapidly in the space of just a few hours, and it was just when you felt you were home and dry that the trouble started. But I had to trust Alia. She'd always been kind and I'd no reason to believe she wouldn't be now. I followed her out of the bedroom, down the stairs and out of the front door towards Grandma's house.

When Grandma saw me, she burst into tears. I stood there in embarrassment, not wanting to cry myself, as she hugged me and promised that I would be safe.

Grandma was a tall, angular old woman who spoke softly but would take no nonsense from anyone. As the light faded outside she lit the wick of a hurricane lamp and turned it up so that its soft glow warmed the room.

'Now,' she said, 'I want you to tell us both exactly what happened. Right from the beginning.'

I told them everything, holding nothing back. Grandma asked many questions and listened carefully, nodding as I detailed the kidnap, life in the madrassa and the escape.

At the end of the account she clasped her bony claw-like old hands around mine. 'I promise you this will never happen again,' she said. 'Boys go to madrassas for many reasons and we were all told that you'd been naughty in England. But that doesn't excuse you being taken away like that. You should've been asked, at least. Aunty Alia has told me that she knew but was unable to prevent it happening.' She shot a look at Alia, who bowed her head in what appeared to be shame. 'Rest assured,' Grandma went on, 'it will not happen again. Anyway, Imran will not find you now, and even if he does, he'll have me to deal with. We are your family and we will take care of you from now on. You know Uncle Hussein is a truck driver, don't you?'

I nodded. Hussein spent a lot of time on the road in his two-storey multi-coloured truck, delivering all sorts of goods across the north of Pakistan. He seemed to love it and would recount funny stories of his life behind the wheel once he'd arrived home.

'Well,' Grandma continued, 'how would you like to spend some time with him in the truck?'

'What, going on journeys and all that?'

I couldn't think of anything more exciting. I would be away from the house and the village and I would get to see some of Pakistan. Plus, Hussein was a good laugh and a kind man. He would look after me. I had visions of the two of us tearing up the highway in his big truck and laughing at some joke or other. I needed a buddy, and Hussein fitted that description perfectly.

'Good,' said Grandma. 'So that is what will happen. It's not right for you to hang around the house with the women and children. How old are you?'

'Thirteen. Nearly 14.'

'Then you're a man, and you can do a man's work. You can start tomorrow, once Imran is out of the way. Now it's about time you were in bed. Imran will be back soon. Go on – on your way.'

Grandma had a powerful presence and I obeyed without question. I couldn't have been happier; I was out of Imran's clutches and finally the family had found me something worthwhile to do. But one thing still nagged me.

'Grandma, when will I be going back to England?'

'Soon,' she said, glancing at Alia, 'very soon, I'm sure. Don't worry about that for now. Go to bed and rest. I'll send Hussein over in the morning, once Imran has gone, to explain everything to you. Goodnight.'

I left, sticking close to Alia as we crossed the courtyard to her house. But there was no sign of Imran. I locked my door, slid into bed and snuggled under the covers.

For the first time in months I felt safe – or safe-ish, given that Imran was on the prowl. But I'd made it. I'd got over that wall, taken the bus to Peshawar, survived in the city and sneaked back to Tajak without anyone seeing me. I felt as though I was my own hero, something I'd never experienced before. I'd found courage out there, and friendship too. I wondered what Abad was doing tonight and whether he was thinking about me. I wished he'd come too, but I understood why he couldn't. Still, I missed him.

Only one thought was nagging me now, apart from Imran finding me: I was a little bit bothered by Grandma's refusal to name a date for my return to England. Still, I was sure that she would be as good as her word and that it would be soon.

Chapter Fifteen

I woke to the sound of the early morning call to prayer from Tajak's mosque. Instinctively I got up and started to put my trousers on. Then I remembered – Imran would also be up and preparing to attend. I didn't like missing morning prayers, but this time I gladly got back into bed. Soon he would be gone.

A few hours later there was a tapping on my door and a deep male voice calling out my name. I froze in horror. Surely he hadn't discovered me at this late stage?

The tapping grew louder, too loud for me to ignore any longer. I turned the key in the lock and opened it, resigned to whatever fate was going to throw at me next.

Before me stood Hussein, smiling broadly beneath his long white Father Christmas beard. He spotted the look on my face and laughed.

'Thought I was Imran, didn't you?! Fooled you! Don't worry, Moham, he's gone. He won't be back for ages, if ever. There's good money to be made in Dubai. That's what he likes. You're safe.'

I didn't return his smile, even though I could've kissed him on the spot. This wasn't a joking matter.

'You knew too, didn't you?'

'Sorry, son,' he said, pulling his beard, 'it was tricky. We only found out at the last minute and we couldn't really stop him. He … was trying to do what he thought was best.'

'For who? Not for me. He had me locked up. That wasn't what was best. I'm not a criminal.'

'I know,' said Hussein, looking sheepish, 'I know. But there was talk, not just here but in England. You were on the wrong path, Moham. It's not good for a Muslim boy to stray. You needed guidance. Maybe Imran's methods were harsh, but …'

'There are no "buts", uncle,' I said. 'He kidnapped me. That's wrong, full stop.'

Hussein nodded.

I couldn't believe that none of them had had the guts to stop Imran in his tracks. Was he really that powerful?

Looking back now, I see that the strings were being pulled from England. It was the people who had moved away who had called the shots. They had the money; they decided what was what. And they'd made up their mind that I needed 're-educating'. Imran was a cruel fanatic, but had he really wielded as much power as it had seemed?

I asked Hussein if it was really true that he'd take me with him as a driver's mate.

'You bet,' he said, pleased that we'd changed the subject. 'I need someone to keep me awake while I'm driving at night.

Anyway, I want to show you something. Get dressed and come downstairs.'

I threw on my stuff and followed him out of the front gate of the compound. There, gleaming as though it had just been hosed down, was a huge 10-wheeler truck. It was two or three storeys high and lavishly decorated all over. A massive amount of effort is put into the decoration of these trucks. The cabin of this one gleamed with shades of gold, silver and emerald inside and out. It was less of a vehicle and more of a mobile work of art. It was long, too; long enough to carry all kinds of goods. I could hardly believe I'd be making this my home on the road.

'Climb up to the top,' said Hussein, delighted that I was impressed. 'You'll see where you'll be sleeping.'

I pulled myself up above the cab using a ladder fixed to the side. Right at the top was a hinged hatch. I opened it and crawled inside. There was no room to stand up, but the space looked very comfortable. It was lined with old rice sacks and goatskins, with richly-decorated cushions scattered around. It was a little palace and I couldn't wait to rest up there as the truck sped through Pakistan.

The truck was owned by a wealthy man in the village who had about five such vehicles. He was a sub-contractor to various companies and would employ men like Hussein to deliver bricks, hay, livestock – whatever was needed.

'I'm off tonight,' Hussein said. 'Do you want to come?'

'I'll go and grab my bag,' I said, scrambling down from the hatch.

Hussein laughed. 'Not for a few hours yet, Moham. First we've got to get some food, and I need to fill her up with fuel. Then we have a good long sleep. When the sun is down and we're refreshed, we go.'

I could hardly wait and mooched around for the rest of the day, hoping that Hussein wouldn't change his mind. But he seemed keen and besides, Grandma had said it would be happening. As noon approached, the household retreated inside. I wondered what they might be saying about me. They'd all know by now that I'd escaped. Were they proud that a member of their family had had the courage to do what I had done? Or were they ashamed of me? Perhaps long truck journeys were a way of keeping that at bay, or at least trying to make up for the guilt they felt. If, indeed, they felt any. Either way, I was too excited to sleep.

Later in the day we ate, and once the plates were cleared away, Hussein said it was time to go.

Our first journey would only be a few hours or so, to a brickworks about 90 miles away. We had to pick up a load of bricks and deliver them to a builder's yard before dawn.

I loved the thrill of sitting in the cab with Hussein, watching the road speed by and listening to his stories. When we arrived at the brickworks we discovered we had to load every single brick by hand. Luckily there were a few guys about who helped us pack and stack, but it was back-breaking work. Like the cane-cutting in Afghanistan I felt that I'd done a proper session of hard graft.

On the way back Hussein let me climb to the top of the cab, which was open, and sit up there. The wind forced me to lie down, but it was wonderful to see dawn breaking over fields, villages and mountains.

On the trips that followed I realized just how beautiful Pakistan was, even though I could never call it home and was still keen to get back to England as quickly as possible.

Hussein even let me drive the truck at one point, though not on my own, I hasten to add. I sat in his lap and steered the vehicle while he operated the pedals. The thought of that happening on one of Britain's busy motorways would fill anyone with horror. In Pakistan it wasn't at all unusual for truckers to show their young sons how to drive.

The roads were dangerous, though, and accidents were common. On one occasion Hussein and I went for a week-long trip to the other side of Pakistan, taking along a co-driver. We had to pick up a huge load of wheat, but towards the end of the journey to the wheat fields Hussein became tired. As he approached the beginnings of a village he was distracted by the sight of a tea stall just up ahead and started to slow down. As he did so, a cyclist emerged from a junction and was clipped by Hussein's truck, which sent him and the bike flying into a nearby wall.

Hussein slammed on the brakes and jumped down to where the cyclist lay motionless. A pool of blood was beginning to form in the dust and as Hussein kneeled over him a crowd gathered, curious to see what had happened.

At first it looked as though the cyclist was dead and gone, but after a few moments he groaned and tried to sit up. He was badly hurt for sure, but within a few minutes he was being carefully lifted into the back of a pick-up truck and taken to hospital.

Inevitably the police showed up and arrested Hussein and his co-driver. They were taken to a small police station in the village. For whatever reason they decided not to interview me, so I sat on the station steps for what seemed hours, waiting for news. Just as I was on the verge of panic, Hussein and his co-driver emerged, looking fraught. They'd been interrogated for ages and the police were keen to nail them for the accident. But it turned out that witnesses had seen the cyclist wobble straight into the path of the truck, so the cops had had no choice but to let them go. Besides, the guy was still alive and would make a good recovery. Such was life in rural Pakistan.

Hussein was keen that we stopped for food at regular intervals and I became addicted to lentil dhal served from the kind of roadside shacks where Hussein and his fellow truckers gathered. I enjoyed hanging around with this group of men who cracked jokes and pulled one another's legs. I felt I could trust them. Their life on the road wasn't an easy one, but they looked after each other and showed great courtesy and respect. It was no wonder, because there were many dangers out there, and not just from wobbling cyclists.

The final trip I took with Hussein, about three or four months after my first, was an overnight journey to deliver rice. There was nothing unusual about it until we reached our destination and were told by the rice merchant that he'd had a call from Hussein's boss. He wanted Hussein to divert into the Punjab province and pick up a load of cement for a building project near Tajak. It was urgent, and as Hussein was already halfway there he could hardly say no. Yet for some reason he was reluctant to make the journey, especially at night. He asked if I would keep chatting as much as possible to keep him awake.

The night was pitch black and the road unlit. All we could see was the truck's headlights in front of us. I must have nodded off, because the next thing I recall was Hussein slowing down. Immediately I felt guilty because I was meant to be keeping him awake. But by the tone of his voice I could tell this was something much more serious.

'Moham, get up to your bed,' he whispered frantically. 'Hurry – now!'

The truck was still moving, but I wasn't going to argue with Hussein. I wound down the cab window and gingerly put my foot on the rung of the ladder up to my bed. The wind caught me and swung me crazily to one side, but I clung on and hauled myself up to the top just as the truck slowed to a stop. Once inside I covered myself with rice sacks and lay as still as possible. Something told me that if I were to be discovered there would be serious trouble.

Below I could hear Hussein speaking in Punjabi to two or three men. He was talking very softly and calmly, which made me even more concerned, as I imagined the people he was dealing with could turn nasty at any moment. I heard the back doors of the truck swing open and a couple of people clamber inside. In seconds the doors slammed shut and the native Punjabi voices went up several notches in volume. They'd obviously found nothing and were furious.

Then I heard a creak at the bottom of the ladder, followed by the sound of someone climbing it. The truck rocked as he hauled himself up. I lay completely still, holding my breath. The hatch opened and I could smell cigarette smoke wafting in. The man looking in shouted something to his mates below and started patting the rice sacks. I inched as far away from the hatch as I could, trying desperately not to make a noise. I felt the cab sway slightly as the man put his knee in. He was about to climb in and have a proper search.

Then, from below, there came the sound of raised voices. The loudest was that of Hussein. It sounded as though he was standing up for himself. An argument broke out and the man withdrew his knee from the cab, climbed down and added his voice to the fray.

I still didn't move a muscle. I wanted to call out to Hussein and find out if he was alright, but something told me to lie quietly until the fracas was over.

After five long minutes the engine coughed into life and we began to move. I wondered who was driving. If it wasn't Hussein, who was it and where were we going?

Twenty-five minutes later I heard the hissing of hydraulic brakes and the truck pulled over gently to the side of the road.

'Moham! Come out. It's safe. Come down and I'll tell you what happened.'

I climbed out and scrambled down the ladder. Hussein was at the bottom and he caught me as I jumped from the final rung.

'Bandits,' he said. 'We were hijacked. This is a dangerous place. They've taken all my money, the bastards. Though it could've been worse …'

'How?'

Hussein wiped his forehead with the sleeve of his grimy shirt. He looked exhausted and frightened.

'A lot of truckers take kids like you with them. Show them what life's like on the road. Sometimes boys are kidnapped. The bandits ask for ransoms. Sometimes they're paid. Sometimes they're not.'

'What happens if they're not?'

'It's probably best you don't know,' he said. 'Come on – let's get this delivery picked up and get out of here. It's not safe.'

Hussein told me to climb back up and hide in the top cab until we'd left Punjab. That made sense, but then he said something I didn't understand – something about not wanting to lose his son-in-law to kidnappers. I curled up under the rice sacks and tried to work out what he meant. A son-in-law, as far as I knew, was someone who was married to a man's daughter. But I was only 13, about to turn 14, and wasn't married to anyone. Hussein was my dad's brother and he had one daughter, Parveen – the little girl who'd been playing in the courtyard when I'd sneaked in from Haqqania. The same girl who'd had a party in her honour at which I was special guest. Ah, so that's what it was! Hussein was making a joke out of that event, when

Parveen had been dressed up like a princess and I had been a kind of prince for her. It was just a game.

I thought no more about it and settled down for what would be a long journey to the cement works and back to Tajak.

The drive passed with no further incident and by the time we reached Tajak the sun was almost up. I was ravenous. I went straight round to Alia's, because I knew she'd be making something for breakfast and didn't want to miss out. Grandma happened to be there and she asked me how the trip had gone.

'Brilliant,' I said. 'It was amazing! We were held up by bandits. They nicked all Hussein's money and they were looking for someone to kidnap. But they didn't find me. I hid under a pile of rice sacks and I didn't move, didn't even breathe. It was so cool!'

I was gushing, as any teenager would in that situation. There was a heavy layer of bravado, too. I wanted to show the family that I could handle danger. I didn't want to admit that I had been shit-scared.

Grandma listened to me in silence, nodding and exchanging looks with Alia. The more I rattled on, the more I became aware that this wasn't what they wanted to hear.

Finally, Grandma put her hand up, cutting me off in mid-flow. 'I think I've heard enough,' she said. 'You won't be going with Hussein again. It's too dangerous.'

'What?! Oh, come on, Grandma, it wasn't that bad. I love going with Hussein. Please ...'

'No. It's final. Too dangerous.'

I argued and pleaded and stamped my foot. I said that I'd been through worse before and could look after myself. I told them that Hussein would fall asleep and crash if I wasn't there to talk to him.

Hussein himself had entered the kitchen as I was arguing my case. 'I'm sorry, Moham,' he said. 'I'll miss you, but it's for the best.'

He obviously knew Grandma wouldn't change her mind.

'But I want to come with you!' I shouted, close to tears now. 'You said I was your son-in-law. So what did that mean then?!'

There was an uncomfortable silence around the kitchen. I stared at each of the three faces in turn. Hussein and Alia looked away in embarrassment.

Grandma spoke. 'It means that you will be married to Parveen one day,' she said. 'You are committed to her. That's why we don't want to lose you.'

'… and also because you're a lovely boy, Moham,' Alia chipped in.

But it was too late. The cat was out of the bag. I stood there speechless, hardly able to believe what I was hearing.

'Hang on, so I'm gonna marry some little kid? Why didn't anyone tell me?'

Grandma looked surprised. 'Well, you went through the engagement ceremony,' she said huffily. 'Didn't you realize?'

Now I was really angry. I had thought these were kind people. But I'd been betrayed, not once but twice. First they'd had me sent to a madrassa to make me more religious. Now I was told that I would be getting married to a child. My cousin.

'No!' I shouted. 'I didn't know! My Pashto was weak then – you knew that. Why didn't you explain to me in English? Yasir could've done it – why do you all lie to me all the time?!'

I ran out of the room, almost ripping the hessian curtain across the door from its hooks. I was blazing bloody mad. I couldn't trust any of them. Why was it always me that seemed to get the shitty end of the stick? Why had I ended up with the relatives from hell?

I sat in the courtyard and cursed and swore and spat. All I wanted was for the clock to go back 10 years to when I had a mum and a dad who were together and happy. Millions of other people had this. It seemed so simple. But it seemed I could never have it. It would always be like this – difficult, annoying, upsetting. It wasn't fair.

From that day I began to withdraw from that family of strangers who fed and accommodated me but seemed to want so much more in return. I steered well clear of Parveen and took no notice of her whatsoever. I knew about arranged marriages, but I had somehow always thought that it wouldn't happen to me. There was no way I'd consider myself engaged to a kid who was hardly out of nappies. That just seemed totally wrong.

In the weeks that followed Alia tried to make amends, as she always seemed to do, but she'd been in on the madrassa incident and now here she was again, keeping secrets about my own life from me. I couldn't hate her – she was too kind – but neither could I trust her. I just wanted to go back to England and I began a campaign of pestering anyone who would listen to see if I could get a leaving date. I was stonewalled all the time, but I wouldn't let up. I'd been a good boy during my time in Pakistan. Now they were going to see another side of me, one that wouldn't stand for much more of this.

I've often noticed that when you're feeling a certain way, people come into your life who reflect those feelings, almost as though they're drawn to you for some reason. I don't think it's a conscious thing; it just happens, in both good and bad ways. During this period of anger, frustration and vulnerability, two such people came into my life.

The first was a male second cousin, Malik. He lived at the other end of Tajak and was an occasional visitor to the compound. I'd seen him a couple of times before I'd been taken to Haqqania, but had had very little to do with him. Yasir had said he was a 'Jack the Lad' and I shouldn't bother with him.

'Why not?' I'd asked innocently. 'He looks OK.'

Malik was about 18 or 19, tall and good-looking, and attracted attention wherever he went. He looked like a laugh, certainly more fun than plain, dumpy Yasir with his thick glasses and chronic mosque habit. Maybe Yasir's disapproval was mixed with jealousy? I didn't know, but I did know that for whatever reason Malik had a bad reputation around Tajak.

A couple of days after I was banned from travelling in the truck Malik showed up at the compound. As usual, he was on the scrounge: money, cigarettes, food – whatever he could get. He had a roguish charm that meant he was usually successful. He'd score a few chapatis or a rupee or two before being sent on his way. He knew to come during the daytime when the men were at work. If they were around, he wouldn't get a bean.

He spotted me skulking in a corner of the courtyard. My days had become boring again – nowhere to go, nothing to do and no indication of when I'd be going back to England. I was feeling angry at the family and sorry for myself. I wasn't in the happiest of places and maybe Malik knew that instinctively. He introduced himself, thrusting out his hand.

'I'm surprised we've not met before,' he said, flashing me his charming grin.

'I was told to keep away from you,' I muttered. I didn't really want to speak to him. I didn't want to speak to anyone.

In response Malik did a little dance, kicking up the dust. 'That's 'cos I'm baaadd, brother,' he laughed, 'just like Michael Jackson! Ever heard of him?'

Of course I had. For some reason Jacko was hugely popular among Asian lads both in England and Pakistan. Western music was hard to come by out there, but there were always bootleg tapes of Michael Jackson for sale. He cut through cultural boundaries like no other artist. Whatever the reason, he was a big star, even in this backwater. As if to prove his devotion, Malik attempted a version of the famous Moonwalk, dragging his *salwar kameez* trousers in the dirt as he did it.

This time, I had to laugh. I'd seen lads in England doing this perfectly in their Nike trainers. Malik's baggy trousers and cheap sandals were no substitute for the real thing, but at least he was having a go. I clapped when he'd finished and he looked pleased.

He perched next to me on the day bed. 'What's up?' he said. 'Aren't you going back to England soon? You should be happy. I would be!'

'I dunno when I'm going back,' I said. 'No one tells me anything round here.'

'Me neither,' he said, lighting a cigarette. 'But I know every-thing. I've got my spies.'

He took a few more puffs on the cigarette then furtively passed it towards me.

'Want some?' he said. 'It's the best you'll get round here ...'

The smell from the cigarette was strange – sweeter and more pungent than the tobacco smoked by the men of the village. I'd no idea what I was being offered and I refused. I didn't like smoking. It reminded me of Imran and Rafiq.

'Suit yourself,' Malik said, taking another hefty drag. 'So ... why are you so bored? What've you been up to?'

I told him about the truck journeys, the nights spent zoom-ing through Pakistan, the food stops, the accident with the cyclist and the near-kidnapping. For some reason he found it all very funny and by the end of my tale I felt like a real co-median. I was pleased to be able to make someone like Malik laugh so hard. The very act of cracking him up had made me feel much better.

'Oh, that's hilarious,' he said, wiping his eyes with his sleeve. 'You're a scream, do you know that? Listen, mate, I'm going in to have a word with Aunty Alia. If you're bored, you can hang around with me. I've always got something going on.'

He got up and went inside, still shaking his head with laughter.

After a while he came out.

'She says it's OK,' he said, tossing his head in the direction of Alia's. 'As long as I don't get you into trouble.' He grinned. 'As if I'd do that …'

As I followed him up the street that day he took great delight in introducing me as his 'British cousin' to everyone he met. Most of them knew who I was, of course, but to Malik, having a Western relative was a boost to his status.

After 20 minutes of walking we came to his house. Round the back lurked a large white dog with strange reddish-brown markings on his paws and head, chained to a post and very ferocious looking.

'Don't go near him,' Malik said dramatically, 'he'll rip your hand off. He's well dangerous.'

The dog barked and strained against the chain. I stepped back in fear as he bared his teeth.

'He's a fighter,' Malik explained. 'I've trained him myself. He could kill any dog round here, no problem.'

I wasn't sure whether to be impressed or not. Dogs weren't a feature of life back in Hawesmill. They were considered dirty and no one kept them as pets. Asian people couldn't understand the English obsession with them. Dogs carried disease, were scavengers and could bite. Nothing else needed to be said.

'Hey, do you want to come to a dog fight? There's one arranged in a couple of weeks. You can see how he gets on. He'll rip the others to bits, I know he will. I'm gonna make some big money out of it.'

I agreed just to please Malik, but in my heart I didn't want to see anything so brutal and bloody. I wasn't squeamish, but the idea of making dogs fight gave me a sick feeling.

Malik told me that the markings on the dog's paws and head were done with henna to give him a warlike appearance. I couldn't understand the mentality of someone who would do that to a dog. Perhaps I was more English than I thought …

After a day or so hanging about with Malik, I realized that the roll-up cigarettes he smoked weren't made of tobacco at all. The friends he introduced me to all followed his example, and while they were careful not to get caught, marijuana didn't seem to be anywhere near as *haraam* as alcohol, which none of them touched. The stuff grew wild in the fields and it appeared to be acceptable enough to smoke it as long as it wasn't obvious. I never touched it, though. Just the smell made me feel queasy and the thought of rolling around the floor, laughing uncontrollably, was weird. But I wasn't under any pressure to try it. Malik's friends knew I was different; not really Pakistani, not truly English. They respected that and left me alone.

However, they were keen to involve me in some kind of animal fight. I made excuse after excuse to avoid seeing a dogfight, but I ended up watching a cockfight that had been arranged in a field outside the village. Malik was behind its organization and involved in the betting side of it. Boys and men gathered in a tight excited circle as two birds, complete with spurs made out of metal pins, squared up to one another and then attacked in a flurry of feathers and high-pitched squawking. It was pretty unpleasant to watch, especially when one bird jammed its spurs into the breast of the other, fatally wounding it. It was more fascinating to watch the crowd: their blood was up and they jumped and danced and roared as the birds tore into each other.

Upset over what I'd seen and scared by the way I'd been drawn in, I walked home through the village in silence. Apart from a bit of cricket on the recreation ground by Hawesmill, I'd never really been a spectator at any sporting event. You could hardly call cockfighting 'sporting', but there was something about the energy of the crowd that was addictive.

Malik's personality was addictive, too. He saw the funny side of everything and was the kind of person it felt good to be around. I didn't mind that he was wild; someone had to take on that role in such a conservative, religious and rural area. Whenever anything went wrong Malik was blamed, but he didn't seem to mind. In fact, he thrived on his reputation.

One afternoon he took me on a short bus ride to a farm beyond the village. We were met by one of the strangest and most unnerving men I'd ever come across. Painfully thin, with a moustache that twisted up at the end, he was what can only be described as a freak. Malik spoke to him in Punjabi. I couldn't understand a word of it, but they were obviously having a very intense conversation. As they spoke, the man's snake-like eyes were fixed directly on me and after a while he indicated that I should sit next to him. Malik commanded me to do it and the man continued talking to him, his arm draped over my shoulder. I felt very uncomfortable indeed and couldn't wait to leave.

On the way home I asked Malik what the conversation had been about. He just said it was 'business', adding that the man 'was a dirty old bugger'.

Some weeks later I was in a barber's shop in Tajak. At the back of the shop was a curtained-off area where local men went to talk, drink tea and smoke. As the barber cut my hair silently I could just about hear the conversation coming from the back room. The men seemed to be talking about nothing in particular – until I heard 'British boy' and 'money'. The words jumped out at me like an electric spark. I caught the barber's eye in the mirror and he looked away, ashamed. Then he went into the back room and the conversation ended abruptly.

I couldn't be sure, but I was convinced they were talking about me. I paid the barber, got on a bike I'd borrowed from Hussein and rode back to the compound as fast as I could.

Malik called round a day or so later, but I made the excuse that I wasn't feeling well. I never saw him again.

The incident only increased my paranoia and misery. Again and again I asked Grandma when I could go home and her reply was always the same: 'I don't know. Sometime soon.'

Lonely and depressed, I began to spend more and more time in my room. I needed something or someone – and what I didn't need was what I was about to get, whether I liked it or not.

Chapter Sixteen

Malik wasn't the only rebel kid in the village. There was another, though this wild child was far less celebrated than the swaggering, pot-smoking, dog-fighting Michael Jackson fan. When this other person's name was mentioned, there would be much eye-rolling and tutting and thanking of lucky stars that they weren't related. If they did happen to be related, my cousin Farida was rarely mentioned at all – at least not in public.

Farida, Little Fatima's daughter, was the striking-looking woman in her mid-twenties who sported plaited pony tails on either side of her head and had quizzed me about England when we first met. Her father was dead and her two sisters were married, so she and her mother lived a quiet existence, cooking and cleaning and generally contributing to the domestic running of the house.

At least, Little Fatima did. Farida was far more reluctant. Baking chapatis and creating fuel from cow dung wasn't really her thing. In another time and place she'd have been a career woman with a loft apartment in a big city and a string of dates in her diary. Sadly for her, she was stuck in a village that squeezed the life out of her high-spiritedness, choking any ambitions she might have had.

All this would have counted for nothing if she'd had a husband. Then, whatever she might have felt inside, she would've been outwardly respectable. But she had no husband. Because of her nature, she wasn't considered a safe bet by village women looking for wives for their sons. Her only chance was in England, but the family didn't seem keen to pack her off there. Probably they thought it was too dangerous for their reputation; she was better off staying in the village where she could be monitored day and night.

I know all this now. Back then, all I saw was an unmarried woman who sang and danced and laughed and made stupid jokes. To be honest, she was an embarrassment, both to herself and her family. I could feel the shame pouring out of Little Fatima and Grandma when Farida said something inappropriate.

There were whispers all around the village about Farida – what she'd done and with whom. Nothing was ever proved, but the rumour-makers didn't care about that.

Up to this point I hadn't had much to do with her; she was a good 10 years older than me and had an odd way of making me feel unsettled. She'd asked me about England a few times and I'd told her bits and pieces about life in Hawesmill. But by and large we had left each other alone.

In the evenings, when the men were at the *baytuk*, the women and children of the compound would gather at Little

Fatima's to watch Indian films on her battered old TV set. I had no idea what these videos were about, but at least it was a form of entertainment. We'd all squat on the floor and laugh along. Sometimes the films would make Little Fatima and Alia cry. Quite often I'd go back to my room halfway through, claiming tiredness – though it was usually boredom. But after the Hussein and Malik incidents I needed cheering up, so I started sitting through to the end. It was during these times that I began to notice Farida looking at me in a strange way.

At first it was a few little smiles and occasional winks. She rarely spoke to me during the film, but would catch my eye and make a gesture. Being polite, I would smile back and carry on watching the film. Then I would look again to see if she was still looking. She usually was, and I would turn away in embarrassment.

She did the same things out in the courtyard. One afternoon she joined me as I was mending a kite.

'Hi, Moham,' she said, winking at me. 'What's going on?'

I told her what I was doing. She sat by me in silence as I carried on fixing it up. I felt uncomfortable, but I finished the job and stood up, ready to take it into the nearby field. Then, quite firmly and without a hint of shame, she pinched my bum.

'Farida! What did you do that for? Bloody hell …'

No one had ever pinched my bum before and it felt totally wrong. And yet strangely exciting too.

'Sorry,' she giggled, 'I couldn't help it. You didn't mind, did you?'

I couldn't say I did and I couldn't say I didn't. I didn't know what to say, so I walked off towards the field. I knew she'd follow me, and I was right.

'Come on, then,' she said as I got ready to launch the kite. 'Show us what you've got.'

'*Huh?*'

'No, you fool – the kite! Get it up in the air!'

I did as I was told and within seconds the kite was soaring high above the flat dry earth. Farida snatched it off me and began running with it. I chased her, knowing she'd do something stupid like let it go. The more I chased, the more she laughed. Then I started laughing too and when I caught her, we collapsed in a hot giggling heap on the clay.

'Right,' she said, panting. 'Your turn ...'

I set off at a cracking pace, but Farida was skinny and athletic. She soon caught up with me and grabbed the string. Then she pinched my bum again and winked, following up with a hefty slap to my arse. I felt like a small child being punished, but I knew this was no punishment. Hot with shame, I turned away and walked back to the compound, leaving her standing alone with the downed kite.

In the days that followed I noticed her more and more, laughing and winking and playing silly games around me. Even if I'd known what flirting was I might not have realized it was happening, but deep down she was stirring feelings in me I'd never known before, even when I'd hung around with the white girls back in Hawesmill. I also knew that she was much older than me and that we were close relations. Something was wrong about this.

One afternoon there was a celebration. A relation at the other end of the village was being married and the party was held in the compound. As usual I was left with the women while the men talked and feasted on the other side of the court-yard. I was 14 now and felt I should join them, but was still at that awkward age – not a child but certainly not a man. Fed up at feeling left in this nowhere-land, I headed off to my room and lay down on the bed.

There was a knock at the door and in came Farida. She had a new outfit on and looked nice. Without asking, she sat down on the side of the bed. I could feel her body touching mine and I moved towards the wall. She noticed and bounced even closer to me, making a little joke out of it.

'Why did you sneak off?' she said. 'Are you bored? I am too. What are weddings like in England? Loads more fun than this, I reckon.'

'Not really. Just the same – eating, talking, whatever. That's it. It's no different.'

''Course it is,' she said, 'you're just pretending. You don't want to hurt my feelings, do you?'

She put out her bottom lip in a pretend sulk, as she often did. Then she laughed.

'Are there loads of pretty girls in England? Have you been with any?'

'No – course not!'

'It's not what I've heard. I've heard you've got a thing about white girls. That's why you were sent over here.'

'I haven't! I don't know any white girls. I only met a couple twice. It wasn't my fault. I didn't chat them up or anything.'

In response Farida put her hand on my arm.

'It's all right, Moham,' she said gently. 'I understand. Girls are girls, wherever they're from. You're a good-looking boy – bet you'll get loads of offers. Anyway, your mum's white, isn't she? It's not surprising you prefer white girls.'

'I don't prefer them,' I said.

Farida smiled. 'Oh. That's good to know. So what kind of girls do you like, Moham?'

'I dunno … I've never really thought about it.'

'Never thought about it?' Farida widened her big brown eyes. 'You must have. Come on …'

Her hand moved away from my arm and came to rest on my inner thigh. She squeezed it gently and suddenly the room felt unbearably hot. I wanted to run out, but although Farida's touch was light I might as well have been in the grip of a wrestler. I was going nowhere.

'Do you like me doing that?' she said, moving her hand a little further up my thigh.

'No … no, not really.'

'Aaahh, you're embarrassed now, aren't you? Never mind. Have a look out of the window, see if the party's getting any better.'

I did as I was told. Nothing much had changed outside. The men were eating hunks of meat and talking. The women were busying themselves around the clay *tandoor* ovens. It could have been a scene from any time in the last 700 years or so.

When I turned round, Farida was sitting there topless.

'Bloody hell, what are you doing?! What if someone comes in?!'

I stared at her breasts, hardly able to believe what I was seeing. It was the first time I'd ever seen a woman topless. I'd never seen any porn magazines or videos and I'd certainly never been that close to naked flesh.

'It's alright,' she said, as if it was the most normal thing on Earth to be semi-naked. 'Do you like them? You can touch them if you want …'

I stared hard at the floor, then looked up again. It wasn't a dream. I was very uncomfortable, but also intrigued.

'I can't,' I muttered. 'I don't want to get into trouble. I've been in enough shit. Please Farida, don't …'

She pulled down her bottom lip and put her top back on.

Outside, the laughter from the men was becoming louder. I had a sudden desire to join them, to get away from temptation. Being around the men would keep me on the right path. I got off the bed and aimed for the door.

Before I made it, Farida caught me by the hand. 'Not today,' she whispered, 'but sometime soon, I promise. You'll like it.'

In the days that followed, the tension between Farida and me was strong. A couple of times I saw Little Fatima looking at her daughter curiously, as if she knew something had happened. But nothing had. I hadn't done anything to provoke

Farida. It wasn't my fault. Maybe Little Fatima knew her daughter too well. Perhaps she also knew that it wouldn't be long before it developed into something more.

It wasn't long before it did. One evening, soon after the wedding, the women and kids were gathered around the telly as usual. I'd had a lot of tea that afternoon and was bursting for a pee. When I came back from the loo, Farida was waiting for me.

'Come on,' she said, grabbing my arm urgently. She was strong and I couldn't have resisted even if I'd wanted to – and I wasn't sure I did.

She led me through the garden to a spot at the back of the property that contained a small grove of orange trees. The air was heavy with the smell of orange blossom and jasmine. She ordered me to lie down under one of the trees and knelt beside me, fiddling with the belt of my trousers and finally pulling them down.

'What are you doing?!' I whispered. 'They'll notice we've gone. Shit, Farida …!'

'Shut up!' There was an urgency in her voice I didn't like but had to obey. 'No one will notice if we're quick.'

She pulled off her own trousers and straddled me, rubbing herself vigorously all over my crotch. All the time she was saying things, stuff that didn't make sense to me. I was scared and curious at the same time. I felt as if I wanted to pee. I don't think I had an erection. Within a couple of minutes Farida made a series of grunting noises then rolled right off me before yanking her trousers up again.

'Right,' she said, her face flushed and her forehead damp, 'we're going back. Oh, and not a word to anyone about this. You don't want to go back to Haqqania, do you?'

'No. Why, will I be going?'

Farida's expression changed. Now she looked hard, determined and cruel.

'You will if you tell anyone. I know people. They'd get good money for taking you back. So keep your mouth shut.'

She marched off, leaving me to do up my trousers. I was totally shocked, both at her shamelessness and the way she'd threatened me. I could tell by her eyes that she meant it.

When I came back into the TV room I made a stupid excuse about getting lost in the dark on the way to the loo. Farida was already back, looking serene. She smiled up at me as though nothing had happened.

I didn't see much of her over the next couple of days and wondered whether the encounter under the orange trees had been a one-off. Then, on the third day, she sidled up to me in the garden as I lay in the shade of the vine.

'Meet me in the far field in 20 minutes,' she whispered, indicating the direction with a flick of her head.

'I can't. I said I'd help Aunty Alia with something.'

'Twenty minutes,' she repeated, fixing me with her hard look. 'Or else … Haqqania.'

I had no choice. Twenty minutes later, just after midday, when everyone else was indoors, Farida and I were wedged together under a tree and she was demanding oral sex. I don't need to go into details, save to say that it was a very weird experience for a 14-year-old boy.

When she'd finished with me that way, she pulled me on top of her, grabbed my backside and pushed me into her, in and out, in and out.

'We're gonna get married, Moham,' she said, grunting. 'Me and you, we're gonna get married and move to England. I want to get away from here. In two years you'll send for me and we'll get married. We can do this all the time then. No one can stop us. You'll take me to England, won't you, Moham? I want to go to England so badly. Come on, come on, come on!'

She was babbling, ranting, saying anything that came into her head as she made me push into her harder and harder. Again I wanted to pee, but in a different way – a very nice, warm way, I have to admit. Eventually I couldn't help myself. I came inside her, my head spinning as all my innocence disappeared in those few strange seconds.

Farida wasn't one for post-coital kisses and cuddles. Once she'd got what she wanted, she was off.

'Thanks,' she said, pulling on her trousers, 'that was good. I can't wait to go to England. Go on, tell me again what it's like.'

I recounted the glossy version of my native country, skipping over the bits about the damp terrace housing, the dull days, the confines of a few dismal streets and the casual racism you got if you set foot outside that ghetto. If she wanted to believe that England was paved with gold, who was I to stop her? It had been the dream of so many immigrants – why would Farida's view be any different?

I imagined being married to her. I had a vision of lots of kids running around while Farida sat in the tiny back room of a Hawesmill house, bored out of her mind and scouting round the neighbourhood youth for a bit of illicit pleasure. Besides, I was already engaged to someone, wasn't I? A child maybe, but the family seemed to think it was all fine. What would my mum think if she knew I was engaged to one cousin and being fucked by another one? It didn't bear thinking about.

Sex with Farida became a daily – sometimes twice and three times daily – business. How she managed to sneak past the watchful eye of her mother, aunty and grandmother and find opportunities for gratification I'll never know. Even if she thought of it, Farida becoming pregnant never even crossed my mind. She was a tremendous risk-taker; the consequences for a woman being caught having sex outside marriage were unthinkable. I would've been punished hard too. At the very least I'd have been sent back to Haqqania, never to return. Farida kept threatening me with that terrible option. Then she'd be nice to me, treating me almost like a boyfriend.

Our relationship was a strange one. Her sex drive was exceptionally strong and she would sometimes hold me down physically to get what she needed. I look back now and wonder how much pleasure she was really gaining from it. I was a totally inexperienced 14-year-old and she was a woman in her midtwenties. The satisfaction level must have been low. Maybe it was more of a control thing, or maybe she was so mindnumbingly bored that any distraction, however wrong, was a welcome one.

All the time she insisted that what we were doing was right, because we would be getting married. I started to believe her. The sex was so frequent that it almost became a normal part of my everyday routine in Tajak. During prayers at the mosque I would silently plead with Allah not to send me to hell, though. I promised Him that Farida and I would be married one day and that would make what we were doing now alright. Once I'd left the mosque I looked forward to sneaking off with Farida. I was becoming addicted to this new pleasure. Was I falling in love? No, I don't think so. But Farida was giving me something that no one else ever had, however quick and rough and wrong it was. There was an unspoken bond between us now.

But the threat of being sent back to Haqqania on Farida's orders also hung over me like a dark cloud. It wasn't long before I realized I was being used and abused. The first was obvious: Farida wanted something and didn't care how she got it. The latter is harder to define. Looking at it today, more than 20 years on, it's obvious that a 25-year-old having sex with a 14-year-old is wrong. It equals a prison sentence. But in rural Pakistan, two decades ago, where cousins routinely married? That's a difficult one. She knew I was vulnerable, I suppose, which is why she took advantage of me. What happened made me feel guilty, especially in the eyes of God, but I can't say I didn't enjoy it. Also, I wondered whether she really meant it about being married, and if she did, would this be my chance to go home to England? She mentioned it so many times that I believed she was sincere, even if all she really wanted was a plane ticket out of there herself.

Alexander Khan

But I never found out. As usual, whispers circulated around Farida and one evening I was confronted by Aunty Alia. She asked me if Farida was bothering me.

'No,' I said, 'not at all. Why do you ask?'

'It's just that she's got a … reputation around here, if you know what that means. She can get a bit silly with the boys. Has that happened at all, Mohammed?'

'No,' I said, the English side of me turning crimson. It was always a giveaway.

'Look me in the eye,' she said, 'and tell me that nothing has been going on between you two.'

'Like what?' I said, trying not to get caught in Alia's sights. She knew that if I were to tell anyone it would be her.

'You're 14 now, Moham,' she said kindly, 'and I think you're big enough to understand what I mean. Now, has she been doing anything to you that you don't like?'

'No,' I said firmly. It was the truth. I didn't like the context of the act or the threat of what would happen if I didn't co-operate, but the act itself … well, yes, I had enjoyed it up to a point.

'Fine,' said Alia, not believing a word of it. 'If she does, I want to know. Alright?'

'Yes, aunty.'

I slunk off, wondering what would happen to us if we were caught. The consequences would be terrible. We'd both be beaten, that's for sure. Maybe she'd suffer a worse fate.

Now I think that Alia was trying to step in before the men of the family found out and applied their own form of justice.

Hussein and Ajmal were nice guys, but they were also traditionalists and the sort of thing Farida and I were up to was deeply disapproved of.

Perhaps Alia and Little Fatima had a word with Farida as well, for when I saw her next she acted very coldly towards me and could hardly say two words, never mind demand sex. I asked her several times what the matter was, but she wouldn't elaborate. She seemed to withdraw into herself, doing the same domestic chores as her mother and aunt without complaining, outwardly at least.

The summer was coming to an end, to be replaced by the cooler wet season. The change in the weather reflected the end of my relationship, if it can be described like that, with Farida – lost, lonely but manipulative Farida who suffered for her reputation and was unable to make any conventional marriage as a result. Marrying her might have been fine for a while, but I think she'd have quickly become bored of life in Hawesmill and started to look for entertainment outside those narrow streets. And who could blame her? When I look back at my own frustrations I can see that Farida and I had a lot in common – two people trying to escape the straitjacket of a highly conventional society. But she was too wild for me, too wild and too old. Before I could find someone I wanted to share my life with, I first had to find myself.

The relationship over, life quickly settled back into its dull village routine. There was no word about leaving for England and any requests I made were met with a 'maybe soon',

'sometime' or 'one day'. There wasn't an ounce of anything definite being offered. In fact the only news about England was the
depressing announcement that in a month's time Aunty Fatima
would be visiting from Hawesmill. As if things weren't bad
enough, I now had to be polite to the woman who had treated
my sister and me so cruelly when we had arrived home from
Pakistan and been put in her care. The thought of seeing her
again made me want to retch. I had little to say to her and I
wondered whether she'd had a hand in sending me to Haqqania.
It was hard to know how she'd take the news of my escape.
Perhaps she already knew and was coming back to make sure I
was returned. I made up my mind that I wouldn't go, even if she
insisted. I'd escape again, but this time I'd get a bus to Islamabad
and catch a plane home. There were only two drawbacks to that
plan – I had no money and my passport had been taken off
me months before and hidden somewhere in the compound.
However, the will was there and sometimes that's all that
counts.

The better news was that my cousin Ayesha was
accompanying Fatima. She had settled down since her secret
radio-listening sessions and was now the mother of two small
children, but she'd always made time for me and been kind and
generous when I'd visited her and Qaisar. They were both good
people in a close-knit world that wasn't always kind, and I
appreciated them for that. Ayesha was still fun. I looked forward
to spending time with her. Maybe I'd be able to persuade her to
talk to the family about me going home. And if I could, perhaps
I'd be able to stay with her and Qaisar for a bit. I'd sleep on a

settee if necessary. Qaisar was religious and he'd make sure I stayed on the straight and narrow. And I'd be able to give Ayesha a hand in the house, taking the kids to the park and playing with them. I saw an ideal family set-up in which I'd be valued and appreciated. I began to tick off the days until Ayesha's arrival.

Meanwhile Farida retreated into herself, becoming moody and nervous looking. What happened to her in the end? I did hear some years ago that finally her wish was granted and she married a man in England, but it went wrong. I hope she's happier now.

Chapter Seventeen

One afternoon, 10 days or so before Fatima and Ayesha's arrival, Aunty Alia approached me with a basket under her arm. It was covered with a rough piece of cloth and something appeared to be wriggling underneath it. I shrank back slightly, thinking one of the men had caught a snake and wanted me to see it. But when she lifted the cloth, a friendly furry little face peeped out. It was a puppy.

'It's for you,' Alia said, softly stroking the dog's head. 'We thought you looked … fed up. Someone found him in the village and we thought you might like a friend.'

She handed the basket over to me. The little dog lifted up his face to be stroked. He had a beautiful white coat. He licked my hand and nibbled my finger. Within seconds he'd found a way into my heart.

I smiled at Alia, who looked pleased to have brought such a precious gift. I'd been spending a lot of time on my own and they must have noticed how isolated I'd become. This was their way of trying to remedy the situation.

I called the puppy Fred, for no other reason than it was the first name that sprang to mind and I wanted something English. I had plans to train him well. He would go everywhere with me. He wriggled in my arms and I kissed his head. For the rest of that day and several days afterwards, we were inseparable.

Then, one morning about a week later, Fred didn't want to come out of his basket. When he was finally coaxed out, something wasn't right. He staggered across the courtyard as though he was drunk and kept lying down. I righted him several times and tried to get him walking, but he just didn't want to go.

I took him to Uncle Ajmal, who was said to have a way with animals. He turned the puppy over in his hands then held him out to me, pointing at the dog's head.

'Look. He's got worms inside his scalp. Maybe they're maggots. Whatever, they're eating his brain. Moham, your dog is very ill.'

Ajmal looked at me pityingly. He knew what he'd said upset me.

'I can try some medicine for him,' he said, 'if you really want ...'

'Anything, Uncle Ajmal. Please ... don't let anything happen to him. He's only little.'

Ajmal went into the house and brought out an old bottle sealed with a wax top.

'We can try this,' he said, applying a yellow liquid to the top of Fred's head.

I'm guessing it was something like iodine; medicines of all descriptions were in short supply and whatever there was certainly wasn't wasted on animals. The idea of a local vet would've been laughable back then. Animals were very low down the pecking order in the typical Pakistani village.

Ajmal told me to wait a day. 'We'll see if he's better then,' he added. 'But if not …'

He didn't need to finish the sentence. I knew what would happen. I stroked Fred and told him I loved him. He nibbled my fingers and wriggled when I tickled his belly. But he clearly wasn't well. His movements were slow and hardly puppy-like. You'd have thought he was at the end of his doggy life, not the beginning.

The following day Ajmal returned to inspect the infection. It hadn't cleared up.

'We can't leave him like this, Moham,' he said, 'that would be cruel. Take him to the corner of the garden, behind the trees. I'll be back in a moment.'

I looked into Fred's eyes as I carried him across the yard. They were sad and full of pain – very much like my own. Everything I did seemed to go wrong. I couldn't even do something as simple as keep a dog without it messing up. I blamed myself for his illness. It was God's way of showing me that I'd misbehaved badly with Farida. I said sorry to Fred and hoped his pain wouldn't last much longer.

Ajmal returned a few moments later with something in his hand. I thought it was some kind of metal pipe, but as he came nearer I saw it was a handgun.

'I'm sorry, Moham,' he said. 'I thought this would be the quickest way. Here,' he held the gun towards me, 'he's your dog. You should do it.'

My hands hung limp by my sides. Had I just heard him correctly? He wanted me to shoot my own dog? He had to be kidding.

'Come on,' he said, with agitation in his voice, 'take the gun. You're a man now, aren't you? Then do it!'

I took the gun out of his hand and he smiled. It was much heavier than I had expected.

Ajmal took the puppy and placed him on the ground. Fred didn't move or try to hide. It was as if he knew what was coming.

'Go on,' Ajmal said, 'point at him, take a deep breath, then squeeze the trigger. We all have to do these things sometimes.'

I pointed the gun at Fred. He looked up at me and my arm swung down by my side again. There was no way I could kill the little animal.

I passed the gun back to Ajmal, who snatched it off me in what appeared to be disgust.

'Away with you,' he said. 'Go back into the house with the women. When you hear a shot you'll know it's done.'

I did as I was told and within a minute it was all over. The shot rang out, echoing around the walls of the compound, and I began to cry.

Alia was baking bread in the kitchen. She put her arm round my shoulders and tried to comfort me, but I shrugged her off. I was supposed to be a man, but I couldn't even do the right thing by my poor dog. The last thing I wanted was the comfort of a woman.

A minute later Ajmal passed the house, the gun in one hand and poor little Fred in the other. He went out by the gate that led to the field and I guessed he would bury the puppy somewhere out there, if he bothered to bury him at all. Dead dogs and cats rarely got the honour of a hole in the ground.

Animals don't have great lives in Pakistan. I once saw a cow slaughtered for a wedding feast and it was one of the most brutal things I'd ever witnessed. The animal was tied to a tree and four men approached it, one holding a huge knife. Somehow they managed to tip it over very quickly and the man holding the knife said a few words of prayer before slitting a huge gash in its throat. Blood spurted everywhere as the cow thrashed around – but not for long. The cut was so deep it almost reached the spinal cord. The cow was left to die in agony before being expertly butchered by the man and his accomplices. It was an incredible sight and whenever I've heard about beheadings carried out by Islamic militants I've thought of that creature, writhing in pain and drowning in its own blood.

Having said that, animals in Pakistan are mostly there for practical use and not to keep as pets. There was no talk of a replacement puppy for me and certainly no mention of me going back to England.

I was alone again. The days slipped back into the old routine – mosque, home, mosque, home, and very little else.

One morning Alia told me that Fatima and Ayesha would be arriving later that day. I didn't react to the news and, head down, simply hurried through Tajak's dusty back streets to the mosque.

The 20-minute walk was eaten up by the image of Fatima's angry, contorted face flashing into my mind. I was older now, but not by much, and she had still the power to frighten me. I could never prove it, but I knew she had been instrumental in sending me here.

The early morning air was cooler than normal and dark clouds hung over the far distant mountains. After months of nothing but relentless baking sun, it felt as though rain was on its way. I climbed the stairs to the mosque and took my usual place by a pillar on the threadbare carpet that covered a marble floor.

As soon as the final verse was finished and the imam had salaamed those gathered, I made my way out and retraced my steps through Tajak, this time at a much slower pace. Fatima and Ayesha wouldn't be here for hours and I didn't want to sit around while the preparations for their visit were taking place. I walked round the village until, out of my mind with boredom, I went back to Alia's and sneaked into my attic room, staying there for the rest of the day.

At around 6 p.m. I could hear shouts of greetings from downstairs. I didn't have to wait long before I was summoned. Alia called for me to come down and I had just enough time to comb my hair and throw on a freshly washed white tunic. I didn't want Fatima to think I was having a bad time here. She would enjoy that, and I wouldn't give her the satisfaction.

'Now, Mohammed,' said Alia with forced jollity, 'say hello to Fatima and Ayesha.'

'Hi,' I said, glancing at them.

They looked pale in comparison to Tajak's sun-baked villagers, especially Ayesha. She also looked thinner and somehow sadder than I remembered. Dark rings had formed under her eyes, and although she smiled and said, 'Hi,' the bubbly personality I knew in Hawesmill appeared to have been well and truly pricked.

Fatima pulled back her sari to reveal a nasty grin that spread across her mouth like a rash.

'Hello, Mohammed,' she said. 'How are you? Behaving, I hope? Alia, if he steps out of line, leave him to me. I'll soon have him on his toes.'

'He's a good boy,' Alia said, taking a protective step closer to me. 'He's been very helpful around the house and he attends mosque five times a day. What more could you ask?'

'He's big enough to work,' Fatima replied, eyeing me up and down, 'now that he appears to be no longer studying. You should find him a job, Alia. Never mind him following you around like a dog.'

Instinctively I looked at Ayesha for support. Once upon a time she'd have made a joke of her mother's methods of discipline and taken me off for a chat, but not now. She stood as still as a statue, her eyes hooded. Something felt distinctly odd. I didn't want to know any more and slunk back to my room, glad to be away from Fatima's quiet malevolence.

Fatima and Ayesha were staying for a month. As far as possible, I kept out of Fatima's way. If she couldn't see me, she couldn't criticize me, so I hid upstairs during the day, reading the Qur'an. I had to eat with Fatima and Ayesha in the evenings, but those meals could hardly be described as festive, despite Alia's best efforts. Every day she put her heart and soul into her delicious pakoras, samosas and highly-spiced curries, but Fatima and Ayesha ate as if they were being given hospital food. I particularly wanted news of Qaisar and whether he'd been to a Test match without me, but when I mentioned his name, the room fell silent. I had a strong feeling that any discussion of him was off-limits, but I didn't know why. I stared at my plate and said nothing.

Ayesha stayed indoors as much as possible, praying constantly, her mother by her side. When she wasn't praying, she was grinding wheat to be made into flour. I tried to speak to her several times when no one else was around, as it was a relief to be able to talk English to someone. I also wondered – though not aloud – if she might be able to help me leave Pakistan and go home. But she was uncommunicative. The most I would get would be a 'yes' or a 'no'. I kept trying to get her attention by mentioning stupid stuff, things like the Ritz crackers she had given me whenever I had visited her. I tried to get her onto the subject of pop music. I even attempted to talk about British TV, which I knew she watched, even though Qaisar disapproved. But every time I tried I was met with near-silence and those dark, hooded and fearful eyes. 'Perhaps', I thought, 'she just hates being with her mum.' Having lived with Fatima myself, I could completely understand that.

As the days wore on, the clouds I'd spotted above the far-off mountains drifted towards Tajak. A dank earthy smell was suddenly present in the air, and the village, so hot and indolent in the daytime, was a hive of activity. The rainy season was about to begin and I couldn't wait. I'm a lad from Lancashire. Rain and damp are in my DNA. At first the sun and high temperatures of rural Pakistan had made a pleasant change. But as time wore on I became sick of the unchanging sky and the constant hiding from the heat. Rain, I thought, would soften some of the harsh extremities of this place. I wanted to feel it on my bare skin, drink it in. I wouldn't have to wait long.

Eight days after Fatima and Ayesha had arrived, I woke to hear a gentle pat-pat on the old woollen blanket strung across my open bedroom window. I stuck my head out to see what was happening. The rain was here. I could've cried with happiness.

For the first time in months I was actually looking forward to morning prayers. I threw on my *salwaar kameez* and rushed out into a street that had become a fast-flowing stream of mud-coloured water. It lapped over my ankles as I sloshed through it. It was like the first snowfall of winter in England and I couldn't have felt happier.

All morning I stayed out in the rain, soaking it up. I helped to push cars out of puddles that had become miniature ponds and escorted elderly people to the local shops. For once I felt a useful member of the village, though the villagers themselves probably thought I was mad. In their opinion the downpour was useful for little more than watering their fields. They couldn't take any pleasure in it at all.

All that activity had made me hungry, so I turned back up the main street towards Alia's with the idea of sneaking in for a bite to eat. Heading towards me, though still relatively far off, was a tall youngish man with a long dark beard, a bag slung over his shoulder. There was something familiar about his loping walk and how he picked his way carefully through the flood-water, as though he was well used to wet streets. I hoped against hope that it was who I thought it was. I waved, and he raised his arm solemnly in greeting. Cousin Qaisar was here.

'Qaisar! Good to see you, man! Where have you been? Why didn't you come out with Ayesha and Fatima? I've missed you. I hope you're stopping around? It's so boring here ...'

'Hello, Mohammed,' he said as he carried on walking. 'Good to see you too. I missed the plane. That's why I'm late.'

Missed the plane? But the others had been here for over a week ... Why had he waited so long to catch another one? I didn't understand, but it didn't matter. He was here now, and at last I had someone to talk to. Delighted, I followed him up the path to Alia's compound.

Then he turned and looked very serious. 'Don't follow me, Mohammed,' he said. 'Wait here.'

He pointed to the ground, as though I was a dog. I was taken aback, and disappointed that he was being so short with me.

'Do I have to? I haven't seen you for ages. Hey, Qaisar, when are we going to the cricket?'

'Soon, Mohammed, soon,' he said irritably. 'Just wait here. Don't come in.'

'OK.'

I turned away from the gate and trudged back into the street. Banished again. Now the rain didn't seem so much fun. I sheltered in a nearby doorway and waited for Qaisar to tell me to come in. Whatever they were talking about obviously wasn't my business.

Suddenly a terrible cracking noise rang out, like a huge tree branch suddenly snapping by my head. In a split-second I was on my knees, my hands grabbing my stomach as if I'd been kicked in the guts. I knew what it was – guns were fired into the air all the time at weddings and parties – but this was so close I could almost taste the smoke from the barrel. What was happening?

A series of screams started from Alia's house, rising up like all the devils in hell. Something terrible had just taken place behind those walls. Despite my sickening fear, I had to find out just what it was. I shoved open the compound gate and ran across the courtyard and up the two steps to the door. The top step was slippery – it was covered in blood that was pouring from under the door and mixing with rainwater to form a deepening pool of horror.

The screaming intensified as I entered the living room, but even that couldn't prepare me for what I was about to see.

Ayesha was writhing in a spasm on the floor, blood pumping from a wound in the side of her head. She was a tall woman and her size seemed to make the thrashing around even more terrifying. Alia and Fatima were screaming, crying and beating their chests. In their midst stood Qaisar. His hair was wet and his expression blank. In his right hand he held a gun. He looked at me, then took aim and fired another round into poor defenceless Ayesha before calmly walking out of the house.

Alia fell on the body sprawled across the floor, kissing the dead woman's bloodied face and vainly cradling her head in her hands. Fatima stood to one side. She had stopped screaming and her expression was as blank and emotionless as that of her daughter's killer. She stared at me icily.

I knew I'd witnessed something I should never have seen. A single thought was spinning around my head: 'Qaisar has killed his wife, Qaisar has killed his wife.' No, not killed – executed. Slaughtered as coolly and ruthlessly as an animal before a wedding ceremony. But why?

I glanced at the floor. My sandals were covered in Ayesha's coagulating blood. I gagged and made for the same door that Qaisar had so nonchalantly walked through.

Fatima grabbed my arm and held it like the bite of a snake.

'Not a word to anyone ever,' she hissed. 'Or the same will happen to you.'

I ran outside. There were people in the compound garden, shouting and screaming. A cousin, a lad just a few years older than me, grabbed my hand. Alia appeared on the step and shouted to him to take me away.

'He saw it!' she screamed. 'He's seen everything! Oh my God, what has happened?! What has happened?!'

By now it was pouring down and I was wet through. My cousin dragged me through the compound gate and up the street.

'Don't kill me!' I pleaded. 'Please don't kill me! I just walked in on it. I'll never say anything about it, I promise!'

I truly believed this young man was simply going to take me round the back of someone's house and shoot me dead.

Instead he told me to shut up and pulled me inside a house, pushing me down onto a cushion. He stood over me, sweating.

'Swear you won't tell anyone!' he shouted. 'Swear it!'

He looked panicked and I knew he could do anything.

'OK, OK,' I said.

He seemed to calm down.

'What happened?' I asked.

'I dunno … I dunno why he did it. She must've …'

'She must've *what*? *What* could she have done that was so bad?!'

The lad ran his fingers through his hair. He looked as scared as I felt. 'She must have dishonoured him – dishonoured the family somehow. That's all I can think of.'

I couldn't imagine how Ayesha could have upset anyone. She'd acted daft and listened to the radio, but that was all in the past. And anyway, it wasn't a crime punishable by death. She had been the kindest person imaginable and I'd just seen her executed in cold blood. The thought made me retch.

The lad's mother made us tea and generally fussed over us. It was clear we were still in shock.

After a couple of hours Alia came over. I'd never seen her looking so dreadful. She was pale and had pulled her *hijab* over her face. She'd obviously been crying hard. I asked her what had happened and why.

She shook her head. 'I can't tell you,' she said. 'Not now, not ever. What you must not do is tell anyone what you saw. That is so important, Moham. You have to promise me.'

I nodded dumbly. I wouldn't tell anyone, simply because I didn't want what had just happened to Ayesha to happen to me. And for more than 20 years I've kept my word, until the writing of this chapter.

I've since been told – and I don't know if it's the truth – that Ayesha was killed because she had been having an affair with someone in Hawesmill and had been found out. To be killed for that is terrible enough, but what haunts me to this day is the thought that she was taken to Pakistan to be murdered and the crime covered up. That couldn't have happened so easily in the UK. To me, that is pure evil.

I never went back to the compound. The lad's mother and Alia agreed I should stay out of the way until the dust had settled. I sat there for two days in shock, replaying the images of the slaying in my mind over and over again. Then Alia came over with some news: I was going home.

It seemed that after months and months of asking on my part, the family had miraculously unearthed my passport and found the fare for my flight. I imagine there was no coincidence about the timing. The Pakistani police might want to talk to any witnesses. As I'd seen Qaisar fire the second shot, I would be a prime candidate for a talking-to down at the station.

Without fuss, and with no goodbye party at the compound gate, I picked up my bag early the following morning and stepped onto the usual rickety old bus for the journey to Islamabad. Alia had said her farewells the previous evening, repeating the warning that I should keep my mouth shut. I was sorry to say goodbye to her; for all that she knew of my abduction to Haqqania and the honour killing of Ayesha, she was a good woman and had been kind to me. I would miss her – but not that much. I was desperate to go home.

Ayesha's death brought home to me once more what a dangerous, unpredictable and wild place I was in. Because of some unspecified 'naughtiness' I'd been sentenced to spend the rest of my teenage years and beyond in a madrassa and no one would've cared if I'd been there forever – people saw it as an honourable and holy place to be. I'd only managed to prevent that through escaping. And if Imran hadn't been leaving the country, if he had caught me – well, what then? Would he have taken me straight back or would he have dispensed the kind of justice that Ayesha received? It was very difficult to tell, especially at that age when so many conflicting emotions are running around your head. I was glad to be getting out, but also felt guilty that it was such a terrible incident that had set me free.

Life in Hawesmill, I decided, would never be as bad as this. I'd learned so much and would make sure that whatever I did with the rest of my life I would be happy that I was no longer locked up in Pakistan, serving a sentence that looked likely to last years and years. I thanked God that I was going home and promised Him that I would always be good and be grateful to Him for releasing me.

Accompanying me home was a young woman from the village who had just got married and was going to England to live with her new husband and in-laws. I had to chaperone her, as was the custom, but we didn't say a lot to each other on the journey to Islamabad. She practically abandoned me on the plane, sitting in the seat opposite, where she spent the time flirting silently with a young guy on the other side of the aisle. She must have known what she was getting into with an arranged marriage in England, but she was still up for a nod and a wink with a handsome stranger. I was older now and a lot wiser, and I could see that human nature was utterly unpredictable, often wild and dangerous. It scared me, and fascinated me too. I wondered what would be waiting for me in England and whether life – and I – would ever be the same again.

Chapter Eighteen

There was a minibus waiting at Heathrow to take me and the new bride back up north to Hawesmill. It had been provided by the groom's family, one of whom was driving it. A few women clustered round the new bride, welcoming her to England. I was nodded at and told to occupy one of the front seats. I didn't say much to the driver over the course of the four-hour journey. I was too busy taking in the country I'd last seen more than two years previously. Trees, fields and houses all sped by in shades of brown and grey, and the further north we got, the more depressing it became. I'd looked forward to this moment for so long; to say it was an anti-climax is an understatement.

Finally we turned off the motorway and followed the main road into Hawesmill. The bus crawled up the long drag of Nile Street, past Fatima's house, and into Hamilton Terrace. We came to a stop outside Abida's. The door opened, my bag was tossed out onto the pavement and I jumped down from the seat, glad to be out of the oppressive atmosphere of the minibus. I watched as it bounced off down the cobbled street. I was home. At last I'd got what I wanted. Or had I?

I knocked on the door. It opened and there stood Rafiq. So he hadn't moved out. I'd hoped he might have gone and found himself a wife, but no, he was still staying with his sister. Who would have a bastard like that anyway? He looked me up and down before allowing me past and into the house. He didn't even say hello.

Abida greeted me with more warmth, even giving me an awkward embrace.

'Welcome home, Mohammed,' she said quietly. 'I hope you'll be happy with us here.'

'Thanks,' I replied.

What more could I say? There was nowhere else to go. Dad was dead, Mum was gone, Ayesha had been murdered and no doubt Qaisar was hiding out in Pakistan until his poor wife had been buried and forgotten about. Fatima wouldn't want me with her, that was for sure. This was home, and I'd just have to get used to it.

A couple of Abida's kids lurked in the background, staring at me. They'd grown a bit, of course, but they still looked little to me.

Jasmine ran downstairs at the sound of my voice. She hugged me and told me she'd missed me.

'It's been so long, Moham!' she squealed. 'I can't believe you're back! I bet you've had loads of adventures. Come on, you've got to tell me everything!'

I smiled. Jasmine had grown too. She was an adolescent now. I wondered whether she'd been promised in marriage to anyone yet. Then I caught Rafiq's gaze.

'It's been … interesting,' I said. 'I'm a bit tired now. I'll tell you about it all sometime soon, I promise.'

Rafiq and Abida exchanged an awkward glance. I'm sure they knew what had happened to Ayesha. I also knew that Rafiq wouldn't dare challenge me about my escape from Haqqania. Between the three of us there was an unspoken trade-off: their silence for mine.

At that point I was happy to be part of the deal. I didn't want to talk about Ayesha anyway. The ordeal was very raw and the image of Qaisar pumping a bullet into her prone body was still going round and round in my mind. I wanted to forget about it, pretend it had never happened. Not talking about it, I decided, would be the best way to deal with it. I was completely wrong, of course. The damage had already been done.

Abida made me something to eat while Jasmine fussed around me, taking my bag upstairs and putting the water on for tea. I asked her what she'd been up to.

'Oh, the same old stuff,' she replied. 'The usual …'

I watched her as she co-ordinated several different tasks in the kitchen without pausing for breath, and I could see she'd been trained very well in the art of the domestic woman.

'Are you going to school now, Jasmine?'

She looked at Abida before answering. 'Nah … not much point, is there? When I get married I won't be rushing off to college or anything. Too much to do at home!'

Abida laughed and she and Jasmine nudged each other, as if to reinforce the position they were both in. I felt sad for Jasmine. Although I'd had many ups and downs in Pakistan, at least I'd had the chance to experience something beyond the confines of these streets. She'd been nowhere and done nothing except cook, clean and keep house. It wasn't fair.

Over the next few days Rafiq grunted a word or two in my direction. He asked me whether I'd been going to mosque and I replied – in perfect Pashto – that I had, and that I'd been very dedicated to my Qu'ranic studies. Even he looked impressed, both with my fluency and my seeming dedication to Islam.

The truth was that I had learned a lot about being a good Muslim while in Pakistan and I'd become devoted to prayer. Perhaps that was because there were things I felt guilty about and hoped Allah would forgive. But I find prayer a great comfort even today, and while I don't go to mosque as much as I did, Islam is still an important part of my life.

So going back to mosque in Hawesmill wasn't a problem, but very quickly I found the routine of life outside the prayer times boring and stifling. I don't know what I expected – in its own way Hawesmill is as conservative as Tajak, or perhaps more so – and things don't change quickly. I didn't quite realize it then, but I was the one who had changed. And dramatically, too. I couldn't express it in words, but I knew I was keen to travel, see the world, mix with other cultures and meet people who didn't automatically have the village mentality. All that would happen in time, and in ways that I could never have predicted. But for the moment I was stuck in the confines of that house and those streets.

Going to school was out of the question. It would've been pointless anyway – I'd hardly been, and to start now would have meant years of catching up. I'm not sure how much time a teacher would have been prepared to spend with a Pakistani boy who could barely spell his own name. Instead, on Rafiq's orders, I was given a job in the shop now owned by Fatima, as Dilawar had died about a year previously.

So I started work in the local shop, and would put in 10-hour days – broken up by visits to the mosque – on a regular basis. The work was mind-numbingly boring. I was allowed to stack shelves and no more – serving customers and taking money was deemed to be beyond me. Tamam worked there too and we managed to have a decent enough relationship; enough for him to ask me about life in Pakistan and to tell me he knew about the madrassa and how I'd got away. Even though he was about 18 by then, he was still impressed by my account of the escape. He never mentioned Ayesha, his sister, of course.

Overseeing the shop business was the one person I really wanted to discuss the time in Haqqania with: Yasir. I wanted to know why the bastard had abandoned me to my fate at Islamabad airport after being so nice to me for weeks beforehand. To me, that had been as cruel as Imran's kidnapping – worse, perhaps, because I'd trusted Yasir and I thought he'd taken me under his wing. Whenever I saw him I felt a burning sense of injustice and the questions I wanted to shout at him lay on the tip of my tongue like a hot chilli. Why did he do that to a young defenceless lad? Was he working under orders? And if so, whose orders were they? I thought I knew the answer to that question, but I had no proof. The family just clammed up and I couldn't get a word out of anyone. Even Tamam wouldn't talk when I asked him who had ordered it. And Yasir himself certainly wasn't saying anything.

In truth, I never asked him. Something about the way he had taken me to Pakistan, so coolly and casually, and then walked away unnerved me. Besides, he was now in charge of the shop and had a lot of power over me. I was in no position to make accusations. He once caught me eating a Cadbury Creme Egg that I'd found dented in the stockroom and gave me an almighty bollocking. It seemed very minor compared to the two years of life that he'd helped steal from me, but as usual I took it without answering back. I wish now that I'd opened my mouth. He had betrayed me in a terrible way and I could never forgive him for it.

Although Rafiq never said as much, it was clear that he resented me being back in Hawesmill. His little plan to keep me in Pakistan forever had backfired spectacularly, but he still ruled the roost in Hamilton Terrace. I avoided him as much as possible. When he and I were in the same room you could almost taste the poison in the air. He could make me feel like shit just by looking at me, and even though he'd almost stopped ranting and raving, he was still an intimidating figure. I hated him, he hated me, and nothing would ever change.

Being in Hawesmill sparked off thoughts about my mum. There were no mysterious knocks at the door now, but I still wondered where she'd gone and whether she would eventually come back for us. One evening when Rafiq was out, I made my way to the top of the house and poked through a few old boxes stored in the bottom of a wardrobe. I knew they contained a few things of Dad's and I wanted something to remember him by. What I found was a set of photographic colour negatives, rolled up tightly and held together with a plastic-coated paper-clip. When I unrolled them and held them up to the bare bulb, I saw the reverse image of a man and a woman. He was in a suit and she appeared to be in traditional Asian dress. The following few frames showed two tiny children by their side. I rolled the negatives up, put them in my pocket and went to find Jasmine. She was mopping the kitchen floor and was reluctant to leave before she'd finished, but I persuaded her to follow me upstairs.

'Who do you think these people are?' I said, unfurling the strip and holding the pictures up so she could see.

'No idea. Grandma and Granddad?'

'Don't think so. He wouldn't wear a suit. I don't know anyone who wears a suit.'

'Get them developed then,' she said, 'or chuck them out. No point keeping rubbish around.'

Poor Jasmine, she was so domestically-minded. I decided to keep them, and out of the pitiful wage I was paid at the shop I saved up enough to have them developed at the chemist's on the other side of the railway line from Hawesmill.

When I picked them up, I almost died of shock. Jasmine and I sat in the top bedroom speechless, just staring at the pictures.

'It's Dad,' she said finally.

'I know.'

'Why's he in a suit?'

'Dunno.'

'Who's that white woman in a sari?'

'Can't you guess?'

Jasmine looked as though she was about to cry.

'I don't remember her, Moham. I can't remember her at all!'

Neither could I. I had a brief flash of dark hair falling across my face as she bent over me, but that was it. But here she was, in full colour, looking happy with her handsome husband, with her two children by her side.

What had happened to that family? Why had it broken up so badly and where was our mum now? I stared at those photos for what seemed like hours that night, and I decided that come what may I would find her one day. I would find her and we would all be together again. My search began that day, a search that would take me 20 years with hardly anything to go on but the fleeting memory of a face.

I asked Jasmine to keep the photos under her pillow. I knew Rafiq didn't trust me and would most likely root through what possessions I had while I was working. A couple of days later I asked Jasmine to get the photos so that I could look at Mum's face again and imprint it on my mind. Jasmine came back, her face flushed. The photos had gone. We never saw them again.

The evidence of a life I'd once led had disappeared, but I was determined that this time I wouldn't allow myself to forget what I had in my mind. I didn't know where to start looking for

Mum, but if I ever happened to leave Hawesmill – on visits to relatives in Blackburn or occasional trips to other mosques around Lancashire – I would look through the minibus windows at the faces of white women in their mid to late thirties and wonder if one of them might be hers.

In the meantime I began to make friends with a few of the local boys. I was now 15 and the trip to Pakistan, despite everything, had actually boosted my confidence with – but not necessarily in – people. When I wasn't working I was no longer content to sit moping in my bedroom, chewing over the past. What had happened in Pakistan had been awful, particularly the ending, but although it was hard to shake off those memories, I knew I had to go forward.

Three lads in particular stood out from the gang of youths who attended mosque. Bashir considered himself a bit of a geezer and tried to act like Al Pacino in *Scarface*. The problem was, he was trying to grow a beard that was very much at the bum-fluff stage. Hamid was much quieter, though with a good sense of humour. His parents were reasonably well-off and his mum was very loud. They had two houses, one of which they lived in while the other was meant to be for someone on benefits who didn't actually exist. So this house was free and Hamid had the key – no wonder lots of teenage lads wanted to be his mate. The final member of this trio was Azam. He had big bulging eyes and was tall and strong for his age. Even then, he wasn't someone to be crossed. He was the wild one, trying to make us all laugh while we prayed.

After mosque, instead of going straight home they'd hang about on the street, talking and cracking jokes. Bashir would smoke fags the teenage way, cupping his hand round the cigarette, taking in deep drags and exhaling the smoke through the corner of his mouth. The three drifted in and out of school without anyone really caring if they were there or not. Hamid's parents were the most concerned about his education, but the nearest any of us really got to school was climbing over the railings in the evening and playing football in the deserted playground.

Little by little I got friendly with these guys, even though I had to take a lot of ribbing from them at first. They found out somehow that my mum was English and would tease me about it unmercifully – 'Your mum's a *kuffar*' and all that type of thing. I took it on the chin because I didn't want to lose their friendship. I told them they didn't understand, and that I'd been to Pakistan and was a better Muslim than any of them anyway. That usually shut them up, because although they'd been for the occasional family visit, none of them had spent any length of time there.

Around this time, towards the end of the 1980s, and especially around the time of the trouble with Salman Rushdie's *Satanic Verses* novel, the messages coming from the preachers in the mosque were of a much stronger flavour than I'd ever heard before. Once the imams had talked about the word of God and obedience to Islamic law; now the sermons were about Westerners: how we shouldn't mix with them at all, how we shouldn't look at white women, how we should keep away from Western food and music, films and books. If we didn't, the punishments from God would be terrifying.

I heard all this in the local mosque and at various other mosques we regularly visited. The preachers read to us in a mixture of Arabic and Pashto or, if they were native to the UK, Arabic and English. A lot of them came over from Yorkshire, places like Dewsbury and Bradford, where there'd been a lot of trouble over the Rushdie book. Sometimes the sermons would be about the life of the Prophet and the beauty of Islam, but more often than not they were filled with hate and anger.

It was during these sermons that the lads' teasing would really start to bite. 'Unbeliever! Unbeliever! Unbeliever!' Bashir would whisper under his breath at me as I tried to listen to what was being said. If it was something about white people and their 'wrong' ways, the teasing would increase tenfold. Looking back, I should've waited until after mosque and given Bashir a smack in the mouth, but I didn't want to lose the only friends I'd got. Besides, the words were beginning to have an effect on me too. Whenever I saw white people I imagined them eating pork and the thought of it knocked me sick. I'd look away from them, hoping not to be tainted by their Western ways. It was ridiculous, especially being half-white myself, but the strength of those preachers' words cannot be underestimated. Certainly, the topic of white people and how they were trying to get rid of Islam was a regular one among us lads – we talked about it far more than we ever talked about girls.

For many months I followed the routine of going to mosque, going to work and hanging about with the lads. Rafiq definitely did not approve of the latter, trying his best to keep me in or pour scorn on those I chose to be friends with. Eventually, though, he came to realize that he preferred the house without me in it and ignored the fact I was staying out later and later.

Oddly enough, it was Abida who tried to put the kibosh on my social life. One evening, as I was approaching my sixteenth birthday, she collared me as I came in from a day at the shop.

'Listen, Moham,' she said, sitting me down in the front room, 'we need to talk about something. You're 16 soon, you know that?'

'Yeah,' I said. 'What are we doing for it?'

'Hmm?'

'Well, are we having a party or what? Other lads do …'

'Oh. Well, no, I wasn't thinking of that exactly.'

'What were you thinking of?'

'More to do with something in Pakistan. Do you remember Parveen, Hussein's daughter?'

Alarm bells began ringing. Parveen was the little kid I'd been 'engaged' to.

'Well, Moham,' Abida continued, 'you're 16 soon and you're of an age when you can marry. She's not very old, I know, but you can have the ceremony in Pakistan and once she's old enough she'll be able to come to England and you'll have a house. How about that?'

How about that? It sounded like a death sentence. I stood up, my face flushed with anger.

'No way!' I shouted, jumping up off the chair. 'No way at all! I'm not doing it. I don't want to get married, not to some kid or anyone else. It's mental! I'm not doing it!'

Abida stared up at me, shocked. 'But it's been arranged,' she said, dumbfounded. 'The family will make it happen. You've been promised to her. That's it.'

I couldn't believe what I was hearing, and told her so. The shouting attracted the attention of Rafiq, who burst in and shoved me back down into the chair, his fist clenched.

'I've heard all that,' he screamed, 'and you won't disobey us! Not now, not ever! You've caused us enough trouble, bastarrd. You will get married to Parveen, and that's final. And if I hear another word from you about it, I'll beat the living daylights out of you. Now get gone!'

He grabbed me by the hair, dragged me out of the room and flung me through the front door onto the street. The speed of his violence never failed to astonish me; he was back inside with the front door slammed shut before I could even begin to consider what an utter twat he was.

I dusted myself off and made my way to Hamid's parents' spare house. I knew the lads would be dossing in there, smoking fags and listening to Pashto music. I went round the back and opened the door. A sweet smell greeted me, the same smell I'd noticed when I'd been with Malik in Pakistan.

Bashir greeted me, a fat joint hanging out of the side of his mouth gangster-style. 'Hey, Moham, what's up?' he drawled, trying to act cool. 'Want some of this?'

I knew by now that it wasn't uncommon for Pathan boys to smoke dope and that while not exactly Islamic, it wasn't particularly frowned on either. But I still wasn't tempted. I was frightened of losing control and being in a bad state of mind in front of Rafiq. So I refused Bashir's offer of a toke – for now.

I told him about Parveen, the arranged marriage and what had just happened in Hamilton Terrace. He laughed and called the others into the kitchen.

'Guess what? Moham's getting wed! To some little kid. What you gonna buy her for a wedding present – a dolly pram?'

They all laughed and I felt ashamed.

'Come on,' said Hamid, 'we're only messing. We're all promised to someone over there, aren't we?'

The others nodded.

'But we've promised each other that it's never gonna happen,' Hamid added. 'Inn't that right, lads?'

They laughed again and I felt better. We were all victims of this mad system of marrying people off way too young. Hamid, Bashir and Azam didn't necessarily object to arranged marriages; they just thought, like me, that 16 or 17 was too young to be promised to someone you'd not met. Like most lads of that age, we didn't want to be tied down. What the others didn't know – because I didn't mention it – was that I'd already had an inkling of how frightening and manipulative and possessive girls could become. Those three, for all their talk, were still as pure as snow. I wasn't, and I certainly didn't want a relationship at that point.

What interested all of us more than talk of marriage and girls was events abroad and the backlash against Muslims following the Salman Rushdie business. From being strange little brown people who ran corner shops and had funny accents, we were all suddenly fanatics and book-burners who handed out death sentences on writers that had offended Islam. The TV news was full of pictures from towns just like ours of heavily-bearded men waving banners and setting fire to effigies of Rushdie. In response, groups like the National Front were becoming stronger again. Life was getting very tense in the towns of northern England, and we kids picked up on it quickly.

That night I didn't go home to Hamilton Terrace, fearing another of Rafiq's rages. Instead I kipped on the floor of the spare house. Hamid, Bashir and Azam also stayed, smoking dope, chatting and playing music. Late in the evening, as I was lying there half-asleep, the orange street light shining straight in through the uncurtained window, I heard all three chanting '*Allah Akhbar!*' ('God is great') over and over again. It seemed an odd phrase to shout and in the morning I asked Bashir what they'd been up to.

'We've got a plan,' he whispered. 'We ain't putting up with this Paki shit from the whites. We've decided – we're going somewhere.'

I thought Bashir was doing his Al Pacino impression yet again, and I laughed. But the look on his face was deadly serious.

'I ain't kidding,' he said. 'There's gonna be trouble in the future. We'll have to know how to fight. We're going abroad – to Pakistan, maybe Afghanistan. You want to come?'

I didn't understand. Why would anyone want to go over there?

'You're so naïve, Moham,' he said, shaking his head. 'We aren't going on holiday.' He leaned in closer. 'There are people round here who know people over there. Holy warriors. They've got these places, out in the desert, where they train kids like us for *jihad*. I ain't kidding. You get given an AK and loads of ammo. It'll be wicked. We're all going. It's sorted. You should come.'

'It's you that's naïve,' I said. 'Remember, I've been over there. You'll regret it. I'm not interested.'

'Suit yourself,' Bashir said with an evil grin, 'you son of a *kuffar*.'

I should've punched his lights out there and then. But he was still my mate, even if he was a nasty little sod. Instead I just laughed and went back upstairs.

I'd seen what went on over there. How they tried to brainwash kids of my age and much younger. How they got people interested in weapons and killing. How life seemed to be cheap, and how limited it was for women. How stuff that was uncomfortable got shoved under the carpet or even buried in the graveyard. For all the talk of respect and family values, I'd seen how people could be betrayed, used and abused. Wild horses wouldn't drag me back to Pakistan and Afghanistan, even if I did feel a tiny bit of sympathy with the idea of bonding with a group of lads and going off to have an adventure somewhere new. If I was ever to do it, it wouldn't be in the name of religion – that much I knew.

I lay on the sagging single mattress in that bedroom and tried to imagine what my future would look like. I couldn't see myself in a training camp with lots of other lads who all looked like me. But I also couldn't see myself in a damp terrace house in the middle of Hawesmill, driving a taxi or working in a curry house while trying to take care of a wife who couldn't speak English and a gaggle of kids who would never go to school and would possess no ambitions beyond the confines of those few streets. I saw myself far away, meeting new people and listening to ideas that would never enter the heads of the people round here. I knew there was something else out there for me, but that it would be a struggle to find it. I had no idea where to begin or who to ask. The people around me had no answers, and even if I'd asked them I'd have been told to shut up and get on with life.

There was also my mum. I sensed she was out there somewhere, waiting for me to find her. I still couldn't understand why she hadn't come back for us, but by now I'd stopped feeling sorry for myself and was determined to do something about it. I wanted to know who she was, what she did, what she stood for, how she lived her life. She must have passed something on to me – what was it, and how would I ever discover it if I didn't make the effort to find her? Whatever values she had, and had passed on, had been buried under a weight of conformity and family pressure. That wasn't the fault of my Asian family – it was just the way they did things. But the only consideration given to my English side was to condemn it as evil. I was sure that couldn't be the case. One day I hoped I'd know the truth.

But for the time being I was still here, and alone once more. My friends had made their decision and within a few weeks they were gone. I was surprised when they left, and admired them for being decisive. But I couldn't agree with them, and I didn't want to set foot in Pakistan again for a long, long time. For one of my friends, the journey there would lead eventually to war and imprisonment. My refusal to go would also lead me into conflict.

All that, however, is a story for another time. For the moment, at least, life for me would go on in its predictable routine. In my head, though, I already had one foot out of those streets and into a world full of possibilities.

'Treat the orphan not harshly,' the Qu'ran says. I had been treated harshly, and there was more to come. But now I was determined to look out for myself and to step into this new world with courage and confidence. If I had no one else to rely on, I would rely on myself alone.

Epilogue

I'm standing on the doorstep of a council house near Hyde, Greater Manchester. It's a rundown area, but the house itself appears to be clean and well kept. I'm wearing my best clothes and my shoes are polished. For former soldiers, old habits die hard.

I'm holding a bunch of flowers. I can hardly breathe. A mixture of emotions is swirling through me: excitement, anticipation, fear. This is the moment I've been waiting for for so many years. I'm praying it will not disappoint.

I knock firmly on the door. Jessica, my wife, squeezes my hand. She knows all about my journey, how I was kidnapped and imprisoned, not just in a madrassa but also by a culture that would not let me explore anything outside its high walls. She knows how I escaped from Pakistan, and from Hawesmill too.

I also explained a lot of it over the phone during the first incredible call I had to a person I thought I'd never see or speak to again. The only possible way of explaining the rest was face to face. So here I am at last. I'm desperate to hear her side, too. She was told we were dead. She didn't believe it, but couldn't prove otherwise.

I hear footsteps across what sounds like a laminate floor. Through the frosted glass I see a pale face framed by long dark hair. A childhood memory – my only memory – of a woman leaning over me, her hair touching my face, comes into focus. It is so long ago and yet I feel three years old again.

A key turns in the lock and a chain is undone. Then the door is opened.

'Mohammed! Oh my Mohammed! It is you – oh my God, it is you!'

The woman just stands there, gazing at me in astonishment. I laugh nervously. She puts a tissue up to her face and starts to cry. I reach for the tissue and gently pull it away.

'Don't cry,' I say, 'it's fine. I'm here now. Move the tissue so I can see you properly.'

She laughs and shoves the tissue into her sleeve. For the first time I really look at her. She is in her middle fifties, small and smartly dressed. She still has the long dark hair I remember. For a moment we just take each other in. Neither can believe this has happened.

Finally, I break the silence. 'What shall I call you – Margaret? Or Mum?'

'It's Mum,' she says, a huge smile on her face. 'It was always Mum. You'd better come in – we've got a lot to talk about.'